SpringerBriefs in Computer Science

For further volumes:
http://www.springer.com/series/10028

Sergio Flesca • Filippo Furfaro • Francesco Parisi

Repairing and Querying Databases under Aggregate Constraints

 Springer

Sergio Flesca
Dipartimento di Elettronica
Informatica e Sistemistica
Università della Calabria
Rende
Italy
flesca@deis.unical.it

Filippo Furfaro
Dipartimento di Elettronica
Informatica e Sistemistica
Università della Calabria
Rende
Italy

Francesco Parisi
Dipartimento di Elettronica
Informatica e Sistemistica
Università della Calabria
Rende
Italy

ISSN 2191-5768
ISBN 978-1-4614-1640-1
DOI 10.1007/978-1-4614-1641-8
Springer New York Dordrecht Heidelberg London

e-ISSN 2191-5776
e-ISBN 978-1-4614-1641-8

Library of Congress Control Number: 2011938682

Printed on acid-free paper

Springer is part of Springer Science+Business Media (www.springer.com)

Preface

It is a common belief that databases and knowledge bases should be completely free of inconsistency. As a matter of fact, commercial database management systems avoid any inconsistency by aborting updates or transactions yielding to an integrity constraint violation. However, this approach for handling inconsistency cannot be adopted in the contexts where knowledge from multiple sources is integrated (such as in the contexts of data warehousing, database integration and automated reasoning systems), since the source giving rise to integrity constraint violation is not clearly identifiable.

A new approach for dealing with inconsistency in contexts such as database integration is that of "accepting" it and providing appropriate mechanisms to handle inconsistent data. The process achieving a consistent state in a database with respect to a given set of integrity constraints can be considered as a separate process that can be executed after that inconsistency has been detected. In other words, the key idea to handle inconsistency is to live with an inconsistent database, and modify query semantics in order to obtain only answers representing consistent information.

Most of the previous work in this area addressed the problem of extracting consistent information from databases violating "classical" forms of constraint (such as keys, foreign keys, functional dependencies). In this manuscript, we focus on databases where the stored data violate a particular form of integrity constraints, called *aggregate constraints*, which define algebraic relationships among aggregate values represented in the database. This kind of integrity constraint can be exploited to impose significant conditions in scientific databases, data warehouses, statistical and biological databases, where the numerical values of some tuples result from aggregating attribute values of other tuples. In this setting, we present a summary of the main results in the research literature on the problem of effectively handling this kind of inconsistency, and present a general framework supporting the extraction of reliable information from databases violating aggregate constraints.

Rende (CS), Italy
August 2011

Sergio Flesca
Filippo Furfaro
Francesco Parisi

v

Abstract Research has deeply investigated several issues related to the use of integrity constraints on relational databases. In particular, a great deal of attention has been devoted to the problem of extracting "reliable" information from databases containing pieces of information inconsistent with regard to some integrity constraints. In this manuscript, the problem of extracting consistent information from relational databases violating integrity constraints on numerical data is addressed. Aggregate constraints defined as linear inequalities on aggregate-sum queries on input data are considered. The notion of repair as consistent set of updates at attribute-value level is exploited, and the characterization of several data-complexity issues related to repairing data and computing consistent query answers is provided. Moreover, a method for computing "reasonable" repairs of inconsistent numerical databases is introduced, for a restricted but expressive class of aggregate constraints. An extension of this method for dealing with the data repairing problem in the presence of weak aggregate constraints which are expected to be satisfied, but not required to, is presented. Furthermore, a technique for computing consistent answers of aggregate queries in the presence of a wide form of aggregate constraints is provided. Finally, extensions of the framework as well as several open problems are discussed.

Keywords Inconsistent databases, aggregate constraints, repairs, consistent query answer, numerical data integrity

Contents

Chapter 1
Introduction

Abstract In this chapter, we make the reader acquainted with the problem of extracting reliable information from databases violating a given set of integrity constraints. After the presentation of the main issues related to repairing and querying inconsistent databases, we introduce the specific problem of repairing and querying numerical databases violating a particular class of integrity constraints (called *aggregate constraints*), whose investigation will be the main topic of the following chapters. Finally, we summarize the related work in the literature dealing with the problem of extracting reliable information from inconsistent databases, and provide a description of the organization of the whole book.

1.1 Dealing with Inconsistent Data

Integrity constraints are the mechanism employed in databases to guarantee that available data correctly model the outside world. Databases may become inconsistent w.r.t. the set of integrity constraints defined for several reasons. Commercial database management systems avoid inconsistency by aborting updates or transactions yielding to an integrity constraint violation. However, often integrity constraints satisfaction cannot be guaranteed by employing this approach. For instance, when knowledge from multiple sources is integrated, as in the contexts of data warehousing, database integration and automated reasoning systems, it is not possible to guarantee the consistency on the integrated information applying the traditional approach. More in detail, when different source databases are integrated, although every source database is consistent with respect to a given set of integrity constraints, in the resulting integrated database many different kinds of discrepancies may arise. In particular, possible discrepancies are due to (i) different sets of integrity constraints that are satisfied by different sources, and (ii) constraints that may be globally violated, even if every source database locally satisfies the same integrity constraints. In this case, there is no update that can be rejected in order to guarantee the consistency of the integrated database as this database instance is not resulting from

S. Flesca et al., *Repairing and Querying Databases under Aggregate Constraints*,
SpringerBriefs in Computer Science, DOI 10.1007/978-1-4614-1641-8_1, © The Author(s) 2011

an update performed on a source database, but from merging multiple independent data sources. For instance, if we know that a person should have a single address but multiple data sources contain different addresses for the same person, it is not clear how to resolve this violation through aborting some update.

The common approach for dealing with inconsistency in contexts such as database integration is that of "accepting" it and providing appropriate mechanisms to extract reliable information from inconsistent data. Specifically, the key idea to inconsistency handling is to live with an inconsistent database, modifying query semantics in order to obtain only consistent information as answers. In fact, when a query is posed on an inconsistent database (according to the traditional semantics) it is possible to yield information which are not consistent with respect to the integrity constraints. Pieces of information contained in an inconsistent database can be reasonably assumed to be consistent if they persist after applying all the possible "minimal" ways of restoring consistency of the database. Here, the term "minimal" means that the restoration of consistency should be accomplished with a minimal impact on the original inconsistent database, trying to preserve as much information as possible. This reasoning is at the basis of two fundamental notions: *repair* and *consistent query answer*. The former is a consistent version of the inconsistent database which is "as close as possible" to the original instance, and the latter consists of the set of answers that can be obtained by posing the query on every repaired database.

The following example describes these two notions in a typical inconsistency-prone data integration scenario: data from two consistent source databases are integrated, and the resulting database turns out to be in an inconsistent state.

Example 1.1. Consider the relation scheme *Teaches*(*Course*, *Professor*), where the attribute *Course* is a key for *Teaches*. Assume there are the following two different instances of *Teaches*:

Course	Professor
CS	Mary
Math	John

Course	Professor
CS	Frank
Math	John

Each of the two instances satisfies the key constraint but, from their union we derive the following inconsistent relation:

Course	Professor
CS	Mary
Math	John
CS	Frank

The above-reported relation does not satisfy the key constraint since there are two distinct tuples with the same value for the attribute *Course*.

We can consider as minimal ways for restoring consistency of the database, i.e. repairs for this database, the following two relations obtained by deleting one of the two tuples that violate the key constraint.

Course	Professor
Math	John
CS	Frank

Course	Professor
CS	Mary
Math	John

On the basis of these alternative repairs, what is consistently true is that '*John*' is the teacher the course '*Math*' and that there is a course named '*CS*'. □

The approach for handling inconsistency described in the example above shares many similarities with the problem of updating a database seen as a logical theory by means of a set of sentences (the integrity constraints). Specifically, given a knowledge base K and a revision α, belief revision theory is concerned with the properties that should hold for a rational notion of updating K with α. If $K \cup \alpha$ is inconsistent, then belief revision theory assumes the requirement that the knowledge should be revised so that the result is consistent. In the database case, the data are flexible, subject to repair, but the integrity constraints are hard, not to be given up.

The "revision" of a database instance by the integrity constraints produces new database instances, i.e. repairs for the original database. Therefore, what is consistently true is what is true with respect to every repaired database. The notion of a fact which is consistently true corresponds to the notion of inference, called *counterfactual inference*, used in the belief revision community. In the database community, the concept of fact which is consistently true has been formalized with the notion of *consistent query answer*, i.e. an answer to a query which results true in every repaired database. Consistent query answer provides a conservative "lower bound" on the information contained in a database.

Example 1.1 (continued). Consider the query $Q(x,y) = Teaches(x,y)$ which intends to retrieve the names of courses with their relative teachers. Obviously, if Q is directly posed on the inconsistent database it returns answers which are consistent with the key constraints and others which are not. On the other hand, the consistent query answers for Q are those which would be returned posing the query in every repaired database, i.e. the tuple $\langle Math, John \rangle$. □

Different repairing primitives can be used for restoring database consistency in reasonable ways. For instance, in the example above, repairs are obtained by performing minimal sets of insertion and deletion of (whole) tuples on the original database, so that the resulting database satisfies the integrity constraints. Another possible notion of repair is that allowing updates of values within some tuples. Considering the example above, this means that the value of the attribute *Professor* in one of the two conflicting tuples must be changed in such a way that a consistent status is obtained. Specifically, we may update either the value '*Mary*' to '*Frank*' in the tuple $\langle CS, Mary \rangle$ or the value '*Frank*' to '*Mary*' in the tuple $\langle CS, Frank \rangle$, obtaining again the two repairs shown in Example 1.1.

In general, different set of repairs can be obtained under different repair notions. Further, since the set of consistent answers to a query posed on an inconsistent database depends on the set of repairs for the database, the repair semantics also alters the set of consistent query answers.

As shown in the following example, when tuples contain both correct and erroneous components the two repair semantics discussed above do not coincide.

Example 1.2. Consider the following database scheme consisting of the relation *Employee*(*Code*,*Name*,*Salary*), where the attribute *Code* is a key for the relation. Assume that the constraint $\forall x, y, z \ \neg[Employee(x, y, z) \wedge z < 10000]$ is defined, stating that each employee must have salary greater than 10000.

For the following (inconsistent) instance of the relation *Employee*, under the repair semantics of deletion/insertion of tuples, there is a unique repair: the empty database instance.

Code	Name	Salary
111	John	1000

On the other hand, if the repaired database is obtained by changing attribute values, there are infinitely many repairs, each of them containing a tuple of the form $\langle 111, John, c \rangle$, where c a constant greater than or equal to 10000.

Thus, under the latter repair notion, the consistent answer to the query asking for the existence of the employee with code '111' is *yes*, whereas under the former repair notion the consistent answer is *no*. This happens because when we delete a tuple containing a wrong component, we also lose the correct components as an undesirable side effect.   □

Several theoretical issues regarding the consistent query answers problem have been widely investigated in literature and some techniques for evaluating consistent answers have been proposed too. The problem of computing consistent answers has been studied among several dimensions, such as the repair semantics, the classes of queries and constraints. Many approaches in literature assume that tuple insertions and deletions are the basic primitives for repairing inconsistent data. More recently, repairs consisting also of value-update operations have been considered. The complexity of computing consistent answers for different classes of first-order queries and aggregate queries has been investigated in presence of several classes of integrity constraints.

In the following section, we introduce the problem of repairing and querying numerical databases violating a particular class of integrity constraints (called *aggregate constraints*), whose investigation is the main topic of this manuscript.

1.2 Numerical Data and Integrity Constraints

Researchers have deeply investigated several issues related to the use of integrity constraints in relational databases. A great deal of attention has been devoted to the problem of extracting reliable information from databases containing pieces of information inconsistent w.r.t. some integrity constraints. Most of the previous work in this area deals with "classical" forms of constraint (such as functional and inclusion dependencies), and proposes different strategies for updating inconsistent data reasonably, in order to make it consistent by means of minimal changes. Indeed, these kinds of constraint often do not suffice to manage data consistency, as they cannot be used to define algebraic relations between stored values. In fact, this issue frequently occurs in several scenarios, such as scientific databases, statistical and biological databases, and data warehouses, where numerical values of tuples are derivable by aggregating values stored in other tuples.

In this book we focus our attention on databases where stored data violate a set of *aggregate constraints*, i.e. integrity constraints defined on aggregate values extracted from the database. These constraints are defined on numerical attributes (such as sale prices, costs, etc.) which represent measure values and are not intrinsically involved in other forms of constraints. The following example describes a real-life scenario where inconsistency of numerical attributes can arise, and aggregate constraints can be exploited to manage the integrity of data.

Example 1.3. The balance sheet of a company is a financial statement providing information on what the company owns (its assets), what it owes (its liabilities), and the value of the business to its stockholders. A thorough analysis of balance sheets is extremely important for both stock and bond investors, since it allows potential liquidity problems of a company to be detected, thus determining the company financial reliability as well as its ability to satisfy financial obligations.

Generally balance sheets are available as paper documents, thus they cannot be automatically processed by balance analysis tools, since these work on electronic data only. Hence, the automatic acquisition of balance-sheet data from paper documents is often performed as the preliminary phase of the decision making process, as it yields data prone to be analyzed by suitable tools for discovering information of interest.

Table 1.1 represents a relation *BalanceSheets* obtained from the balance sheets of two consecutive years of a company. These data were acquired by means of an OCR (*Optical Character Recognition*) tool from paper documents. Values '*det*', '*aggr*' and '*drv*' in column *Type* stand for *detail*, *aggregate* and *derived*, respectively. Specifically, an item is *aggregate* if it is obtained by aggregating items of type *detail* of the same section, whereas a *derived* item is an item whose value can be computed using the values of other items of any type and belonging to any section. This example will be referred to as "Balance Sheets" and used as a running example. We will denote the i-th tuple in Table 1.1 as t_i.

Relation *BalanceSheets* must satisfy the following integrity constraints:

κ_1:for each section and year, the sum of the values of all *detail* items must be equal to the value of the *aggregate* item of the same section and year;

κ_2:for each year, the *net cash inflow* must be equal to the difference between *total cash receipts* and *total disbursements*;

κ_3:for each year, the *ending cash balance* must be equal to the sum of the *beginning cash* and the *net cash inflow*.

Although the original balance sheet (in paper format) was consistent, its digital version is not, as some symbol recognition errors occurred during the digitizing

	Year	Section	Subsection	Type	Value
t_1	2008	Receipts	beginning cash	drv	50
t_2	2008	Receipts	cash sales	det	900
t_3	2008	Receipts	receivables	det	100
t_4	2008	Receipts	total cash receipts	aggr	1250
t_5	2008	Disbursements	payment of accounts	det	1120
t_6	2008	Disbursements	capital expenditure	det	20
t_7	2008	Disbursements	long-term financing	det	80
t_8	2008	Disbursements	total disbursements	aggr	1220
t_9	2008	Balance	net cash inflow	drv	30
t_{10}	2008	Balance	ending cash balance	drv	80
t_{11}	2009	Receipts	beginning cash	drv	80
t_{12}	2009	Receipts	cash sales	det	1110
t_{13}	2009	Receipts	receivables	det	90
t_{14}	2009	Receipts	total cash receipts	aggr	1200
t_{15}	2009	Disbursements	payment of accounts	det	1130
t_{16}	2009	Disbursements	capital expenditure	det	40
t_{17}	2009	Disbursements	long-term financing	det	20
t_{18}	2009	Disbursements	total disbursements	aggr	1120
t_{19}	2009	Balance	net cash inflow	drv	10
t_{20}	2009	Balance	ending cash balance	drv	90

Table 1.1 Relation *BalanceSheets*

phase. In fact, constraints κ_1, κ_2 and κ_3 are not satisfied on the acquired data shown in Table 1.1:

i) for year 2008, in section *Receipts*, the aggregate value of *total cash receipts* is not equal to the sum of detail values of the same section: $900 + 100 \neq 1250$;

ii) for year 2009, in section *Disbursements*, the aggregate value of *total disbursements* is not equal to the sum of detail values of the same section: $1130 + 40 + 20 \neq 1120$;

iii) for year 2009, the value of *net cash inflow* is not equal to the difference between *total cash receipts* and *total disbursements*: $10 \neq 1200 - 1120$.

□

In the literature, two minimality criteria are generally employed for assessing the reasonableness of a repair, namely the *set-* and *card*-minimality. Both these semantics aim at giving an insight on the extent to which the repair preserves the information represented in the original database. Specifically, a repair ρ is said to be *set*-minimal [resp., *card*-minimal] if there is no repair ρ' such that ρ' is a strict subset of ρ [resp., ρ' contains fewer updates than ρ]. Initially, starting from the seminal work [4], the research community has devoted its attention mainly to the use of the *set*-minimal semantics, for different classes of integrity constraints. However, more and more interest has been exhibited in the *card*-minimal semantics in recent works: repairs with the minimum number of performed updates were first used in [28] (where a strategy for fixing categorical data was introduced), then discussed in [7] (in the context of relational data violating specific forms of universal constraints), and, finally, studied in more detail in [43], in the presence of denial constraints.

The interest in both the *set*- and *card*-minimal semantics, in the presence of different forms of integrity constraints, is due to the fact that, depending on the particular scenario addressed, each of them can be more suitable than the other. Also in the presence of aggregate constraints (like those of Example 1.3), these semantics are suitable for different application contexts. For instance, in the scenario of Example 1.3, where inconsistency is due to acquisition errors, repairing the data by means of sets of updates of minimum cardinality seems more reasonable, since the case that the acquiring system made the minimum number of bad symbol-recognition errors can be considered the most probable event. The same reasoning can be applied to other scenarios dealing with numerical data acquired automatically, such as sensor networks. In this case, inconsistency is often due to some trouble occurred at sensors while generating some reading, thus repairing data by modifying the minimum number of readings is justified. On the other hand, the *set*-minimal semantics appears to be more suitable in the data integration context, where assembling data from different (even consistent) databases can result in an inconsistent database (see [40] for a survey on inconsistency in the context of data integration).

Besides the minimality semantics adopted, the repairing strategies proposed for traditional forms of constraints differ in the update operations allowed for fixing the inconsistent data. Most of the work in the literature considers repairs consisting of tuple insertion/deletion operations on the inconsistent database. Indeed, this repairing strategy is not suitable for contexts analogous to that of Example 1.3, that is of data acquired by OCR tools from paper documents. In fact, using tuple insertions/deletions as basic primitives means hypothesizing that the OCR tool skipped/"invented" a whole row when acquiring the source paper document, which is rather unrealistic. In this scenario, a repairing strategy based on attribute-update operations only seems more reasonable, as updating single attribute values is the most natural way for fixing inconsistencies resulting from symbol recognition errors. The same holds in other scenarios dealing with numerical data representing pieces of information acquired automatically, such as sensor networks. In a sensor network with error-free communication channels, no reading generated by sensors can be lost, thus repairing data by adding new readings (as well as removing collected ones) is of no sense. However, also in the general case, as observed in [48], a repairing strategy based on value updates can be more reasonable than strategies performing insertions and/or deletions of tuples. In fact, aggregate constraints are defined on *measure attributes* only, i.e., numerical attributes which are often a small subset of the whole set of attributes. Hence, deleting tuples to make the data consistent has the side-effect of removing the (possibly consistent) information encoded in the other attributes of the deleted tuples, thus resulting in a loss of information which is avoided if only value updates are allowed. On the other hand, a repairing strategy using tuple insertions suffers from the problem that often there is no reasonable way to guess the values which should be assigned to the non-measure attributes in the tuples to be inserted.

This book provides a study of the problem of extracting reliable information from databases violating a set of aggregate constraints in a setting where an attribute-level repairing strategy is adopted. Before presenting the organization of the book, a brief overview on the main issues and results in the area of inconsistent databases is provided.

1.3 Overview of Inconsistency Handling in Databases

Although first theoretical approaches to the problem of dealing with incomplete and inconsistent information date back to 80s, these works mainly focus on issues related to the semantics of incompleteness [37]. The semantics of queries posed on inconsistent integrated databases was first investigated in [3], where an extension of relational algebra (namely *flexible algebra*) was proposed to evaluate queries on data inconsistent w.r.t. key constraints. An extension of the the flexible relational model, called *integrated relational model*, was proposed in [19] where it was argued that the semantics of integrating inconsistent data is captured by the *maximal consistent subset* (with *null* values) of the integrated data. In [42] a different semantics (namely, *merging by majority rule*) based on the *cardinality* of the source databases containing the same tuples was introduced in order to manage data inconsistent w.r.t. first-order integrity constraints.

The first proof-theoretic notion of *consistent query answer* was introduced in [14], expressing the idea that tuples involved in an integrity violation should not be considered in the evaluation of consistent query answers. In [4] a different notion of consistent answer was introduced, based on the notion of *repair*: a repair of an inconsistent database D is a database D', on the same scheme as D, satisfying the given integrity constraints and which is minimally different from D. Thus, the consistent answer of a query q posed on D is the answer which is in every result of q posed on each repair D'. In particular, in [4] the authors show that, for quantifier-free conjunctive queries and binary universal constraints, consistent answers can be evaluated without computing repairs, but by looking only at the specified constraints and rewriting the original query q into a query q' such that the answer of q' on D is equal to the consistent answer of q on D. The query-rewriting technique introduced in [4] was further developed in [16] where an implementation of the rewriting operator is also presented. Later the query-rewriting technique was extended in [31, 29] to work for a subclass of conjunctive queries with existential quantification in the presence of key constraints. Recently, the this technique was further studied in [51, 52].

Starting from the notions of repair and consistent query answer introduced in [4], the problems of repairing and querying inconsistent databases were investigated in several works where more expressive classes of queries and constraints were considered. The complexity of the consistent query answer problem in the presence of both functional and inclusion dependencies was studied in [15] and in [18, 17] under different repair-semantics. Specifically, in [15] it was shown that for key and inclusion dependencies the consistent query answers problem is undecidable if repairs consisting of both insertions and deletions of tuples are considered. Decidable cases were identified by limiting the interaction between the two type of dependencies: either considering inclusion dependencies that are *non-key-conflicting* or considering *key consistent* databases. In [18, 17] the computational complexity of the consistent query answer problem was further investigated in the presence of both denial constraints (a class of integrity constraints which includes that of functional dependencies) and inclusion dependencies for several classes of queries with existential quantification under the assumption that data are complete (thus exploiting a repairing strategy using tuple deletions only). The notion of *range-consistent answer* which extends that of consistent answer in order to handle aggregation queries was introduced in [6, 8], where the complexity of the range-consistent query answer problem was investigated for aggregation queries (without grouping) in the presence of functional dependencies. Aggregation queries with grouping were subsequently investigated in [30], where a rewriting algorithm for computing range-consistent answers was proposed.

Several works exploited logic-based approaches to address both the problem of computing repairs and that of evaluating consistent query answers. In fact, repairs can be represented as *answer sets* of logic programs with disjunction and classical negation [5, 7, 11, 36, 35], and consistent query answers can be evaluated by exploiting skeptical reasoning in these logic programs. Specifically, in [5, 7] repairs were specified by means of *disjunctive logic programs with exceptions* with e-answer set semantics. These logic programs can be transformed into extended disjunctive logic programs (without exceptions) with answer set semantics, and then further transformed into equivalent disjunctive normal logic programs with stable model semantics [34]. In [36, 35] repairs were specified by means of *extended disjunctive logic programs* derived from the set of integrity constraints. Moreover, *repair constraints* expressing conditions under which repairs are feasible, and *prioritized update rules* giving preference to some repairs for the database with respect to others, were introduced. It was shown that both universal integrity constraints and repair constraints can still be rewritten into extended disjunctive logic programs which specify repairs for a database, but the introduction of prioritized updates requires the use of *prioritized extended disjunctive rules* [47]. In [9], a repairing framework based on a non-classical logic (the *annotated predicate calculus* [38]) was proposed, which works for queries that are conjunctions or disjunctions of positive literals in the presence of universal constraints. This strategy was extended in [10] to deal with referential integrity constraints. A similar approach was proposed in [11], where repairs were specified as the stable models of a disjunctive logic program where the database predicates contain *annotations* as extra arguments (as opposed to annotated programs that contain annotated atoms). This approach works for first-order queries in presence of universal and referential integrity constraints.

All the above-cited works assume that the basic primitives for repairing inconsistent data are tuple insertions and deletions. Repairs consisting of also updating attribute values were considered in [28, 12, 13, 48, 49, 50]. In particular, [48] was the first investigating the complexity of the consistent query answer problem in a setting where the basic primitive for repairing data is the attribute-value update. Although the basic primitive used to find a repair is that of updating attribute values, repairs consisting of also tuple insertions and deletions can be obtained in [48, 49, 50]. In [50] it was shown that for full dependencies and conjunctive queries, repairs for a database can be summarized into a single tableau called *nucleus* for the database. As a consequence, the consistent answers of conjunctive queries can be evaluated by looking at the nucleus only.

[28, 12, 13] mainly focus on the problem of computing repaired databases rather than evaluating consistent query answers. This problem is relevant in several contexts, where users are interested in a consistent version of the data on which an analysis task can be accomplished (a context where users need to perform such tasks is introduced in Section 1.2). In [28], the computation of repairs was studied for categorical data in the presence of constraints expressed as first order formulas. Specifically, the DLV system [41] was exploited for computing repairs w.r.t. first-order constraints expressing edit rules of questionnaires collecting census data. In [13], repairs on categorical data in the presence of functional and inclusion dependencies were studied, and a cost model for computing database repairs as set of value modifications was introduced. The authors observed a strong connection between the database repairing area and the *record linkage* field (also known as *duplicate removal* or *merge-purge*), which refers to the task of linking pairs of records that refer to the same entity in different data sets [20, 54]. This connection between searching for a repair for an inconsistent database and the record linkage task also motivates the automatic computation of repairs. The problem of checking whether a repair is reasonable according to a minimality criterion (namely, *repair checking problem*) was addressed in [2], where several repair minimality semantics were investigated.

In [12] the problem of repairing databases by fixing numerical data at attribute level was addressed. The authors introduced the notion of Least-Square repair minimizing the square Euclidean distance between the original and repaired database instance, and shown that deciding the existence of Least-Square repairs under both denial constraints (where built-in comparison predicates are allowed) and a non-linear form of multi-attribute *aggregate constraints* is undecidable. Then they disregarded aggregate constraints and focused on the problem of repairing data violating denial constraints, where no form of aggregation is allowed in the adopted constraints. After providing some intractability results, it was shown that for *local* denial constraints, Least-Square repairs can be computed by solving particular instances of the *Minimum Weighted Set Cover Optimization Problem* that admit approximation within a constant factor.

Aggregate constraints on numerical data was first investigated in [46], where the consistency problem of very general forms of aggregation was considered, but no issue related to data-repairing was investigated. The form of aggregate constraints considered in this book was introduced in [22], where the complexity of several problems regarding the extraction of reliable information from inconsistent numerical data (i.e. repair existence, minimal repair checking, as well as consistent query answer) was investigated. In [25] the problem of repairing and querying database inconsistent w.r.t. aggregate constraints was further investigated. In [21], the architecture of a tool for acquiring and repairing numerical data inconsistent w.r.t. a restricted form of aggregate constraints was presented, along with a strategy for computing reasonable repairs, whereas in [23] the problem of computing reasonable repairs w.r.t. a set of both strong and *weak* aggregate constraints was addressed. The problem of querying inconsistent numerical databases was further investigated in [24, 27], where techniques for evaluating aggregate queries were presented.

1.4 Organization

This book provides an overview of the research done in the context of repairing and querying databases inconsistent w.r.t. a given set of aggregate constraints. The manuscript is organized as follows. In Chapter 2, the notion of repair as consistent set of updates at attribute-value level, as well as that of consistent query answer is defined. This notions are then exploited in Chapter 3, where the characterization of several data-complexity issues related to repairing data and computing consistent query answers is provided. Next, in Chapter 4 a method for computing reasonable repairs of inconsistent numerical databases is introduced, for a restricted but expressive class of aggregate constraints, namely *steady aggregate constraints*. An extension of this method for dealing with the data repairing problem in the presence of aggregate constraints with *weak* semantics is also presented. In Chapter 5, a technique for computing consistent answers of aggregate queries in the presence of steady aggregate constraints is presented. Many of the results presented in Chapter 3, 4 and 5 can be studied in depth in [22, 21, 23, 25, 24, 27]. Finally, extensions of the framework as well as several open problems are discussed in Chapther 6.

Chapter 2
Preliminaries

Abstract We here introduce the notions which are fundamental for dealing with the problem of extracting reliable information from (inconsistent) data in the presence of aggregate constraints. Specifically, we formalize the basic concepts of *aggregate constraint*, *repair*, *repair minimality*, and *consistent answer*, which will be exploited in the following chapters to define a general framework for repairing and querying inconsistent numerical data. We also provide a brief overview of the complexity classes which will be referred to when addressing the complexity characterization of several problems related to the above-mentioned framework.

2.1 Basic Notations

We assume classical notions of database scheme, relation scheme, and relation instances. In the following we will also use a logical formalism to represent relational databases, and relation schemes will be represented by means of sorted predicates of the form $R(A_1:\Delta_1,\ldots,A_n:\Delta_n)$, where R is said to be the name of the relation scheme, $A_1,\ldots,A_n$ are attribute names (composing the set denoted as $\mathscr{A}_R$), $\Delta_1,\ldots,\Delta_n$ are the corresponding domains, and n is said to be the arity of R. Each Δ_i can be either $\mathbb{Z}$ (infinite domain of integers), $\mathbb{Q}$ (rationals), or $\mathbb{S}$ (strings). For the sake of brevity, relation schemes will be often identified by their names (thus omitting their signature consisting of attribute names and domains).

A tuple over a relation scheme R of arity n is a member of $(\mathbb{Z}\cup\mathbb{Q}\cup\mathbb{S})^n$ [1]. A relation instance of R is a set r of tuples over R. A database scheme $\mathscr{D}$ is a set of relation schemes, whereas a database instance D is a set of relation instances of the relation schemes in $\mathscr{D}$. Given a tuple t, the value of attribute A of t will be denoted as $t[A]$.

Given a boolean formula β consisting of comparison atoms of the form $X \diamond Y$, where X, Y are either attributes of relation scheme R or constants and $\diamond$ is a compar-

---

[1] This definition of tuple over a relation scheme admits tuples inconsistent w.r.t. attribute domains.

S. Flesca et al., *Repairing and Querying Databases under Aggregate Constraints*,
SpringerBriefs in Computer Science, DOI 10.1007/978-1-4614-1641-8_2, © The Author(s) 2011

ison operator in $\{=, \neq, \leq, \geq, <, >\}$, we say that a tuple t over R satisfies β (denoted as $t \models \beta$) if replacing the occurrences of each attribute A in β with $t[A]$ makes β true.

Domains $\mathbb{Q}$ and $\mathbb{Z}$ will be said to be *numerical domains*, and attributes defined over $\mathbb{Q}$ or $\mathbb{Z}$ will be said to be *numerical attributes*. Given a relation scheme R, we will denote the set of its numerical attributes representing measure data as $\mathcal{M}_R$ (namely, *measure attributes*). That is, $\mathcal{M}_R$ specifies the set of attributes representing measure values, such as weights, lengths, prices, etc. For instance, in "Balance Sheet" example, $\mathcal{M}_R$ consists only of attribute *Value*. Given a database scheme $\mathcal{D}$, we will denote as $\mathcal{M}_{\mathcal{D}}$ the union of the sets of measure attributes associated with the relation schemes in $\mathcal{D}$.

On each relation scheme R, a key constraint is assumed. Specifically, we denote as $\mathcal{K}_R$ the subset of $\mathcal{A}_R$ consisting of the names of the attributes which are a key for R. For instance, in "Balance Sheet" example, $\mathcal{K}_R = \{Year, Subsection\}$. We also denote the key of a relation scheme by underlining its key attributes. Throughout this book, we assume that $\mathcal{K}_R \cap \mathcal{M}_R = \emptyset$, i.e., measure attributes of a relation scheme R are not used to identify tuples belonging to instances of R. Although this assumption leads to a loss of generality, it is acceptable from a practical point of view, since the situations excluded by this assumption are unlikely to occur often in real-life scenarios. Clearly, this assumption holds in the scenario considered in "Balance Sheet" example.

We distinguish among measure and non-measure attributes as, in our framework, we will rely on the assumption that inconsistencies involve measure attributes only, whereas non-measure attributes are assumed to be consistent. Therefore, also key constraints are assumed to be satisfied. The rationale of this assumption is that, in many real-life situations, even if integrity violations of measure data can coexist with integrity violations involving non-measure data, these inconsistencies can be fixed separately. For instance, in the balance sheet scenario of our running example, errors in the OCR-mediated acquisition of non-measure attributes (such as lacks of correspondences between real and acquired strings denoting item descriptions) can be repaired in a pre-processing step using a dictionary, by searching for the strings in the dictionary which are the most similar to the acquired ones. In fact, in [21], a system prototype adopting such a dictionary-based repairing strategy for string attributes is described. The study of the problem of repairing the data when these different forms of inconsistencies cannot be fixed separately is left as an open issue and it will be discussed together other possible extensions in Chapter 6.

2.2 Domain Constraints and Aggregate Constraints

Several forms of constraints can be defined over a database scheme restricting the set of its valid instances. In this book we deal with two forms of constraints: *domain constraints* and *aggregate constraints*. The former impose that, if an attribute is associated with a domain Δ in the definition of a relation scheme, then it must take value from Δ. The latter define algebraic relationships among measure attributes, and are formally defined in what follows.

An *attribute expression e* on R is either a constant or the name of a numerical (either measure or non-measure) attribute of R. Given an attribute expression e on R and a tuple t over R, we denote as $e(t)$ the value e, if e is a constant, or the value $t[e]$, if e is an attribute.

Given a relation scheme R and a sequence $\mathbf{y}$ of variables, an *aggregation function* $\chi(\mathbf{y})$ on R is a triplet $\langle R, e, \alpha(\mathbf{y}) \rangle$, where e is an *attribute expression* on R and $\alpha(\mathbf{y})$ is a (possibly empty) boolean combination of atomic comparisons of the form $X \diamond Y$, where X and Y are constants, attributes of R, or variables in $\mathbf{y}$, and $\diamond$ is a comparison operator in $\{=, \neq, \leq, \geq, <, >\}$. When empty, α will be denoted as $\perp$.

Given an aggregation function $\chi(\mathbf{y}) = \langle R, e, \alpha(\mathbf{y}) \rangle$ and a sequence $\mathbf{a}$ of constants with $|\mathbf{a}| = |\mathbf{y}|$, $\chi(\mathbf{a})$ maps every instance r of R to $\sum_{t \in r \wedge t \models \alpha(\mathbf{a})} e(t)$, where $\alpha(\mathbf{a})$ is the (ground) boolean combination of atomic comparisons obtained from $\alpha(\mathbf{y})$ by replacing each variable in $\mathbf{y}$ with the corresponding value in $\mathbf{a}$. We assume that, given a relation R and an aggregation function χ on R, if the condition α of χ is not satisfied by any tuple in the instance of R, then χ returns 0.

Example 2.1. The following aggregation functions are defined on the relation scheme *BalanceSheets (Year, Section, Subsection, Type, Value)* of Example 1.3, where $\mathscr{K}_{BalanceSheets} = \{Year, Subsection\}$, $\mathscr{M}_{BalanceSheets} = \{Value\}$, and the measure attribute *Value* ranges over domain $\mathbb{Z}$:

$$\chi_1(x,y,z) = \langle BalanceSheets, Value, (Section=x \wedge Year=y \wedge Type=z) \rangle$$
$$\chi_2(x,y) = \langle BalanceSheets, Value, (Year=x \wedge Subsection=y) \rangle$$

Function χ_1 returns the sum of *Value* of all the tuples having *Section x*, *Year y* and *Type z*. Basically, $\chi_1(x,y,z)$ corresponds to the following SQL expression:

```
SELECT sum(Value)
FROM   BalanceSheets
WHERE  Section=x AND Year=y AND Type=z
```

For instance, evaluating χ_1('Receipts', '2008', 'det') on the relation instance shown in Table 1.1 results in $900 + 100 = 1000$, whereas χ_1('Disbursements', '2008', 'aggr') returns 1220. Function χ_2 returns the sum of *Value* of all the tuples where *Year=x* and *Subsection=y*. In our running example, as the pair *Year, Subsection* is a key for *BalanceSheets*, the sum returned by χ_2 is an attribute value of a single tuple. For instance, χ_2('2008', 'cash sales') returns 900, whereas χ_2('2008', 'net cash inflow') returns 30.   □

Definition 2.1 (Aggregate constraint). Given a database scheme $\mathscr{D}$, an aggregate constraint on $\mathscr{D}$ is an expression of the form:

$$\forall \mathbf{x} \left(\phi(\mathbf{x}) \implies \sum_{i=1}^{n} c_i \cdot \chi_i(\mathbf{y}_i) \leq K \right) \tag{2.1}$$

where:

1. n is a positive integer, and $c_1, \ldots, c_n, K$ are constants in $\mathbb{Q}$;
2. $\phi(\mathbf{x})$ is a (possibly empty) conjunction of atoms constructed from relation names, constants, and all the variables in $\mathbf{x}$;
3. each $\chi_i(\mathbf{y}_i)$ is an aggregation function, where $\mathbf{y}_i$ is a list of variables and constants, and every variable that occurs in $\mathbf{y}_i$ also occurs in $\mathbf{x}$.

The semantics of an aggregate constraint is the "natural" one, that is, given a database instance D over the database scheme $\mathscr{D}$, an aggregate constraint of the form (2.1) imposes that, for all the substitutions θ of the variables in $\mathbf{x}$ with constants of D making $\phi(\theta(\mathbf{x}))$ *true*, the inequality $\sum_{i=1}^{n} c_i \cdot \chi_i(\theta(\mathbf{y}_i)) \leq K$ holds on D.

Observe that aggregate constraints enable equalities to be expressed as well, since an equality can be viewed as a pair of inequalities. For the sake of brevity, in the following, equalities will be written explicitly.

Example 2.2. The constraint κ_1 defined in Example 1.3 can be expressed as follows:

$$\forall\, x, y, s, w, v\ BalanceSheets(y, x, s, w, v) \implies \chi_1(x, y, \text{`det'}) - \chi_1(x, y, \text{`aggr'}) = 0\ \square$$

For the sake of simplicity, in the following we will use a shorter notation for denoting aggregate constraints, where universal quantification is implied and variables in ϕ which do not occur in any aggregation function are replaced with the symbol '_'. For instance, the constraint of Example 2.2 can be written as:

$$BalanceSheets(y, x, \_, \_, \_) \implies \chi_1(x, y, \text{`det'}) - \chi_1(x, y, \text{`aggr'}) = 0$$

Example 2.3. The constraints κ_2 and κ_3 of Example 1.3 can be expressed as follows:

$$\kappa_2 : \quad BalanceSheets(x, \_, \_, \_, \_) \implies \chi_2(x, \text{`net cash inflow'}) - $$
$$(\chi_2(x, \text{`total cash receipts'}) - \chi_2(x, \text{`total disbursements'})) = 0$$

$$\kappa_3 : \quad BalanceSheets(x, \_, \_, \_, \_) \implies \chi_2(x, \text{`ending cash balance'}) -$$
$$(\chi_2(x, \text{`beginning cash'}) + \chi_2(x, \text{`net cash inflow'})) = 0$$
$$\square$$

The following examples show additional usages of aggregate constraints.

Example 2.4. Consider the database scheme $\mathscr{D}$ resulting from the integration of the three source databases consisting of the following relation schemes, respectively:

$R_1(\underline{Year}, Costs)$
$R_2(\underline{Project}, \underline{Year}, Costs)$
$R_3(\underline{Project}, \underline{Month}, \underline{Year}, Costs)$

where $\mathscr{M}_{R_i} = \{Costs\}$, for each $i \in [1..3]$.

The above-introduced three relations come from three distinct sources, each of them containing information about the costs of the projects developed by a university, with different level of granularity. Specifically, the central administration of the university received and maintained in R_1 the total yearly costs of the projects, while the business offices of the faculty and the department received and stored the costs of each project aggregated per year and month, respectively in R_2 and R_3. In particular, the costs in R_1 and R_2 took into account both the equipments and the pays of the employees, while in R_3 only the sums of the pays of the employees were reported.

Consider the following constraints:

κ_a : for each project, the yearly cost for equipments and salaries must be greater than or equal to the sum of the monthly costs for salaries in the same year;

κ_b: for each year, the overall cost for equipments and salaries must be equal to the sum of the yearly costs for equipments and salaries for the different projects.

The above constraints can be expressed as follows::

$$\kappa_a : \quad R_2(x,y,\_) \implies \chi_3(x,y) - \chi_4(x,y) \geq 0$$

where:

$$\chi_3(x,y) = \langle R_2, Cost, (Project = x \wedge Year = y) \rangle$$
$$\chi_4(x,y) = \langle R_3, Cost, (Project = x \wedge Year = y) \rangle$$

$$\kappa_b : \quad R_1(y,\_) \implies \chi_5(y) - \chi_6(y) = 0$$

where:

$$\chi_5(y) = \langle R_1, Cost, Year = y \rangle$$
$$\chi_6(y) = \langle R_2, Cost, Year = y \rangle.$$

□

Example 2.5. Consider the database scheme consisting of the relation schemes $R_1(\underline{Department}, Area)$, and $R_2(\underline{Project}, Department, Costs)$. In R_1, each department is associated with a research area, and, in R_2, each research project is associated with the department in which it was developed and its overall costs. Consider the following integrity constraint: *for every project developed in a department of the 'database' area, the costs must be less than or equal to 100K.* This constraint is expressed by the following aggregate constraint: $R_1(x, \text{'database'}) \wedge R_2(y,x,\_) \implies \chi(y) \leq 100K$, where $\chi(y) = \langle R_2, Cost, Project = y \rangle$. □

Example 2.6. Consider a relation instance over the relation scheme *Employee(Name, Salary, Bonus)*, where both *Salary* and *Bonus* are measure attributes. Consider the constraint requiring that *a total amount of 30K of bonuses has been distributed among the employees receiving a salary greater than 5K.* We can express this constraint by means of the aggregate constraint $\implies \chi() = 30K$, where $\chi() = \langle$ Employee, Bonus, $(Salary > 5K) \rangle$ returns the sum of bonuses for the employees whose salary is greater than 5K. □

Observe that, according to Definition 2.1, the conjunction of atoms on the left-hand side of an aggregate constraint can be empty. Thus, an expression of the form $\implies \chi(k_1, \ldots, k_q) \leq K$, where $k_1, \ldots, k_q$ are constants, is an aggregate constraint, whose semantics derives from assuming the left-hand side of the implication true. In the following, for the sake of readability, we will omit the symbol '$\implies$' for this form of constraint. For instance, the aggregate constraint introduced in Example 2.6 can be written as $\chi() = 30K$.

2.3 Numerical Database Inconsistency

According to the two above-defined forms of constraint on numerical data (domain and aggregate constraints), we consider two forms of database inconsistency. Specifically, given a database instance D over the database scheme $\mathscr{D}$, we say that D *is inconsistent w.r.t.* $\mathscr{D}$ if D contains a tuple t over a relation scheme $R(A_1:\Delta_1,\ldots,A_n:\Delta_n)$ of $\mathscr{D}$ such that, for some $A_i \in \mathscr{M}_R$, it holds that $t[A_i] \notin \Delta_i$. Moreover, given a set of aggregate constraints $\mathscr{A}\mathscr{C}$ on $\mathscr{D}$, we say that D *is inconsistent w.r.t.* $\mathscr{A}\mathscr{C}$ if there is an aggregate constraint $ac \in \mathscr{A}\mathscr{C}$ (of the form (2.1)) such that there is a substitution θ of variables in $\mathbf{x}$ with constants of D making $\phi(\theta(\mathbf{x}))$ *true* and the inequality $\sum_{i=1}^{n} c_i \cdot \chi_i(\theta(\mathbf{y}_i)) \leq K$ *false* on D. We will write $D \not\models \mathscr{A}\mathscr{C}$ (resp., $D \not\models \mathscr{D}$) to denote that D is inconsistent w.r.t. $\mathscr{A}\mathscr{C}$ (resp., w.r.t. $\mathscr{D}$), and $D \models \mathscr{A}\mathscr{C}$ (resp., $D \models \mathscr{D}$) otherwise.

2.4 Steady aggregate constraints

In this section we introduce a restricted form of aggregate constraints, namely *steady aggregate constraints*. On the one hand, steady aggregate constraints are less expressive than (general) aggregate constraints, but, on the other hand, we will show in Chapter 4 that computing a *card*-minimal repair w.r.t. a set of steady aggregate constraints can be accomplished by solving an instance of a Mixed Integer Linear Programming (MILP) problem [33]. This allows us to adopt standard techniques addressing MILP problems to accomplish the computation of a *card*-minimal repair. It is worth noting that the loss in expressiveness is not dramatic, as steady aggregate constraints suffice to express relevant integrity constraints in many real-life scenarios. For instance, all the aggregate constraints introduced in "Balance Sheet" example can be expressed by means of steady aggregate constraints.

Let $R(A_1,\ldots,A_n)$ be a relation scheme and $R(x_1,\ldots,x_n)$ an atom, where each x_j is either a variable or a constant. For each $j \in [1..n]$, we say that the term x_j is *associated* with the attribute A_j. Moreover, we say that a variable x_i is a *measure variable* if it is associated with a measure attribute.

Definition 2.2 (Steady aggregate constraint). An aggregate constraint ac on a given database scheme $\mathscr{D}$ is said to be *steady* if the following conditions hold:

1. for every aggregation function $\langle R, e, \alpha \rangle$ on the right-hand side of ac, no measure attribute occurs in α;
2. measure variables occur at most once in ac;

3. no constant occurring in the conjunction of atoms ϕ on the left-hand side of ac is associated with a measure attribute.

Specifically, condition (2) of Definition 2.2 implies that measure variables cannot occur in the argument $\mathbf{y}_i$ of an aggregation function χ_i appearing in ac. Intuitively, this means that no condition is imposed on measure variables, which can be viewed as "placeholders". Definition 2.2 implies that, for a given database instance D and a steady aggregate constraint ac on the scheme of D, the tuples in D which are "involved" in ac (i.e. the tuples where both ϕ and α of the aggregation functions in ac evaluate to true) can be detected without looking at measure attribute values. As will be clearer in the following, this property allows us to translate ac into a set of linear inequalities, and then express the computation of a *card*-minimal repair w.r.t. ac and the database scheme as an instance of MILP problem. Basically, the reason why such a translation works is that the above-discussed properties of steady aggregate constraints ensure that repairing the inconsistencies will not create new inconsistencies.

Example 2.7. Consider the constraint κ_1 of "Balance Sheet" example (defined in Example 2.2). It is easy to see that this constraint is steady. In fact:

- the formula α of the aggregation function χ_1 on the right-hand side of the constraint contains no occurrence of measure attributes;
- the unique measure variable v does not occur as argument of χ_1 and it does not appear in any other conjunct on the left-hand side of the constraint;
- no constant is associated with a measure attribute on the left-hand side of the constraint.

Similarly, it is straightforward to see that constraints κ_2 and κ_3 of "Balance Sheet" example are steady too.   □

Observe that also the constraints introduced in Example 2.4, as well as those of Example 2.5, are steady. In the following example, instances of aggregate constraints which are not steady are discussed.

Example 2.8. Consider the database scheme introduced in Example 2.5, containing the relation scheme $R_2(\underline{Project}, Department, Costs\,)$, and the following constraint: *There is at most one "expensive" project* (a project is considered expensive if its costs are not less than 20K). This constraint can be expressed by the following aggregate constraint: $\chi() \leq 1$, where $\chi = \langle R_2, 1, (Costs \geq 20K) \rangle$. As attribute *Costs* is a measure attribute of R_2, and it occurs in the formula α of the aggregation function χ, the above-introduced aggregate constraint is not steady (condition (1) of Definition 2.2 is not satisfied).

Analogously, the aggregate constraint introduced in Example 2.6 is not steady. □

2.5 Repairs

The concept of repair is fundamental to define a strategy for extracting reliable information from inconsistent databases. In this section, we introduce repairs consisting of sets of updates at attribute-level that will be used for fixing inconsistent numerical databases.

Definition 2.3 (Atomic update). Let $t = R(v_1, \ldots, v_n)$ be a tuple over the relation scheme $R(A_1 : \Delta_1, \ldots, A_n : \Delta_n)$. An *atomic update* on t is a triplet $< t, A_i, v_i' >$, where $A_i \in \mathcal{M}_R$ and v_i' is a value in Δ_i and $v_i' \neq v_i$.

Update $u = < t, A_i, v_i' >$ replaces $t[A_i]$ with v_i', thus yielding the tuple $u(t) = R(v_1, \ldots, v_{i-1}, v_i', v_{i+1}, \ldots, v_n)$. We denote the pair $< tuple, attribute >$ updated by u as $\lambda(u)$, that is $\lambda(u) = < t, A_i >$. Observe that we consider atomic updates working on the set $\mathcal{M}_R$ of measure attributes only, since, as explained in Section 2.1, non-measure attributes are *a priori* assumed to be correct.

Definition 2.4 (Consistent database update). Let D be a database instance and $U = \{u_1, \ldots, u_n\}$ be a set of atomic updates on tuples of D. The set U is said to be a *consistent database update* iff $\forall j, k \in [1..n]$ if $j \neq k$ then $\lambda(u_j) \neq \lambda(u_k)$.

Informally, a set of atomic updates U is a consistent database update iff, for each pair of updates $u_1, u_2 \in U$, either u_1 and u_2 work on distinct tuples, or they change different attributes of the same tuple.

The set of pairs $< tuple, attribute >$ updated by a consistent database update U will be denoted as $\lambda(U) = \cup_{u_i \in U} \{\lambda(u_i)\}$.

Given a database instance D, a tuple t in D, and a consistent database update U, we denote the tuple obtained by applying the atomic updates in U of the form $< t, A, v >$ on t as $U(t)$. Moreover, we denote the database instance resulting from applying all the atomic updates in U on the tuples of D as $U(D)$.

We now introduce the notion of repair for a database w.r.t. a set of constraints.

Definition 2.5 (Repair). Let $\mathcal{D}$ be a database scheme, $\mathcal{AC}$ a set of aggregate constraints on $\mathcal{D}$, and D an instance of $\mathcal{D}$. A *repair* ρ for D w.r.t. $\mathcal{D}$ and $\mathcal{AC}$ is a consistent database update such that $\rho(D) \models \mathcal{D}$ and $\rho(D) \models \mathcal{AC}$.

Example 2.9. The database instance in the "Balance Sheet" example can be made consistent w.r.t. the set of integrity constraints defined in Examples 2.2 and 2.3 by increasing the values of attribute *Value* of both t_2 and t_{18} up to 1150 and 1190, respectively. That is, $\rho_1 = \{ \langle t_2, Value, 1150 \rangle, \langle t_{18}, Value, 1190 \rangle \}$ is a repair.   □

2.6 Card- and Set-minimal Repairs

We will show in Chapter 3 that the problem of deciding whether there is repair for a database violating a given set of aggregate constraints is decidable. In particular, we show that this problem belongs to the class of the problems that can be decided in polynomial time w.r.t. the size of the database by a Turing machine with an *NP* oracle.

In general, if a database can be repaired, different repairs can be performed on *D* yielding a new database consistent w.r.t. $\mathscr{D}$ and $\mathscr{AC}$, although some of them may not be considered "reasonable". For instance, if a repair exists for *D* changing only one value in one tuple of *D*, any repair updating all values in all tuples of *D* can be reasonably disregarded. To evaluate whether a repair should be considered "relevant" or not, we introduce two different ordering criteria on repairs, corresponding to the comparison operators '$<_{set}$' and '$<_{card}$'. The former compares two repairs by evaluating whether one of the two performs a subset of the updates of the other. That is, given two repairs ρ_a, ρ_b, we say that ρ_a precedes ρ_b ($\rho_a <_{set} \rho_b$) iff $\lambda(\rho_a) \subset \lambda(\rho_b)$. The latter ordering criterion states that a repair ρ_a is preferred w.r.t. a repair ρ_b ($\rho_a <_{card} \rho_b$) iff $|\lambda(\rho_a)| < |\lambda(\rho_b)|$, that is if the number of changes issued by ρ_a is less than ρ_b.

Observe that $\rho_a <_{set} \rho_b$ implies $\rho_a <_{card} \rho_b$, but the vice versa does not hold, as it can be the case that repair ρ_a changes a set of values $\lambda(\rho_a)$ which is not a subset of $\lambda(\rho_b)$, but whose cardinality is less than that of $\lambda(\rho_b)$.

Example 2.10. Consider the repair ρ_1 for "Balance Sheet" example introduced in Example 2.9, and the repair $\rho_2 = \{t_2, Value, 1000\rangle, \langle t_3, Value, 250\rangle, \langle t_{18}, Value, 1190\rangle\}$. It is easy to see that $\rho_1 <_{card} \rho_2$ and $\rho_1 <_{set} \rho_2$.   □

Definition 2.6 (Set- and card-minimal repairs). Let $\mathscr{D}$ be a database scheme, $\mathscr{AC}$ a set of aggregate constraints on $\mathscr{D}$, and *D* an instance of $\mathscr{D}$. A repair ρ for *D* w.r.t. $\mathscr{D}$ and $\mathscr{AC}$ is a *set*-minimal repair [resp., *card*-minimal repair] iff there is no repair ρ' for *D* w.r.t. $\mathscr{D}$ and $\mathscr{AC}$ such that $\rho' <_{set} \rho$ [resp. $\rho' <_{card} \rho$].

Example 2.11. The repair ρ_1 of Example 2.9 is minimal under both the *set*-minimal and the *card*-minimal semantics.
Consider the repair $\rho_3 = \{\langle t_2, Value, 1150\rangle, \langle t_{15}, Value, 1060\rangle, \langle t_{19}, Value, 80\rangle, \langle t_{20}, Value, 160\rangle\}$. The repair ρ_3 is minimal only under the *set*-minimal semantics. It is not *card*-minimal since, for instance, ρ_1 consists of fewer atomic updates.
Now, consider the repair $\rho_4 = \{\langle t_2, Value, 1150\rangle, \langle t_{15}, Value, 1000\rangle, \langle t_{18}, Value, 1060\rangle, \langle t_{19}, Value, 140\rangle, \langle t_{20}, Value, 260\rangle, \}$. The strategy represented by ρ_4 can be reasonably disregarded, since the atomic updates of repair ρ_3 or those of repair ρ_1 suffice to make *BalanceSheets* consistent. In fact, ρ_4 is not minimal both under the *set*-minimal semantics (as $\rho_3 <_{set} \rho_4$) and under the *card*-minimal one (as $\rho_1 <_{card} \rho_4$).   □

Given a database scheme $\mathscr{D}$ and a database instance *D* of $\mathscr{D}$ which is not consistent w.r.t. a set of aggregate constraints $\mathscr{AC}$, different *set*-minimal repairs (resp., *card*-minimal repairs) may exist for *D*. The sets of *set*- and *card*-minimal repairs of *D* w.r.t. $\mathscr{D}$ and $\mathscr{AC}$ will be denoted as $\rho^{set}_{\mathscr{D},\mathscr{AC}}(D)$ and $\rho^{card}_{\mathscr{D},\mathscr{AC}}(D)$, respectively.

Example 2.12. In the "Balance Sheet" example, $\rho^{card}_{\mathscr{D},\mathscr{AC}}(D) = \{\rho_1, \rho_5\}$ where ρ_1 is the repair defined in Example 2.9 and $\rho_5 = \{\langle t_3, Value, 350\rangle, \langle t_{18}, Value, 1190\rangle\}$. The set $\rho_{\mathscr{D},\mathscr{A}\mathscr{C}}^{set}(D)$ for our running example contains ρ_1, ρ_3, ρ_5 and further *set*-minimal repairs, such as $\rho_3 \setminus \{\langle t_2, Value, 1150 \rangle\} \cup \{\langle t_3, Value, 350 \rangle\}$.

2.7 Consistent Answers

We address the problem of extracting reliable information from data violating a given set of aggregate constraints. Specifically, we consider boolean queries checking whether a given tuple belongs to a database, and adopt the widely-used notion of consistent query answer introduced in [4]. More complex forms of queries will be considered in Chapter 5, and further extensions to different forms of queries will be discussed in Chapter 6.

Definition 2.7 (Query). A *query* over a database scheme $\mathscr{D}$ is a ground atom of the form $R(v_1, \ldots, v_n)$, where $R(A_1, \ldots, A_n)$ is a relation scheme in $\mathscr{D}$.

Given a query q issued on a database D, we write $q \in D$ (resp., $q \notin D$) if q evaluates to *true* (resp., *false*) on D.

Definition 2.8 (Consistent query answer). Let $\mathscr{D}$ be a database scheme, D an instance of $\mathscr{D}$, $\mathscr{A}\mathscr{C}$ a set of aggregate constraints on $\mathscr{D}$ and q a query over $\mathscr{D}$. The *consistent query answer* of q on D under the $\mathscr{S}$-minimal semantics (denoted as $q_{\mathscr{D},\mathscr{A}\mathscr{C}}^{\mathscr{S}}(D)$, with $\mathscr{S} \in \{set, card\}$) is true iff for each $\rho \in \rho_{\mathscr{D},\mathscr{A}\mathscr{C}}^{\mathscr{S}}(D)$ it holds that $q \in \rho(D)$.

Observe that, according to the above-reported definition, in the case that a database D does not admit any repair, the consistent answer of any query on D is true (under both the *set*- and *card*- minimal semantics).

Example 2.13. Consider the query $q= BalanceSheet(2009, Disbursements, total disbursements, aggr, 1190)$. It is easy to see that the consistent answer of q under the *card*-minimal semantics is *true*, as this ground tuple belongs to every database repaired by a *card*-minimal repair in $\rho_{\mathscr{D},\mathscr{A}\mathscr{C}}^{card}(D) = \{\rho_1, \rho_5\}$. However, the consistent answer of q under the *set*-minimal semantics is *false*, since $q \in \rho_1(D)$ but $q \notin \rho_3(D)$, where ρ_1 and ρ_3 are the *set*-minimal repairs introduced in Examples 2.9 and 2.11, respectively.

2.8 Complexity Classes

In the following chapters, we study the computational complexity of several problems related to evaluation of repairs and consistent answers. Our complexity results refer to the *data complexity* assumption [1], which measures the complexity of a problem as a function of the size of the database instance, while the database scheme, the query and integrity constraints are assumed to be fixed.

We will consider the following complexity classes [39, 45]:

- *PTIME*: the class of decision problems which are solvable in polynomial time by deterministic Turing Machines. This class is also denoted as P;
- *NP*: the class of decision problems which are solvable in polynomial time by nondeterministic Turing Machines;
- co*NP*: the class of decision problems whose complements are in *NP*;
- Σ_2^p: the class of decision problems which are solvable in polynomial time by nondeterministic Turing machines with an *NP* oracle. This class is also denoted as NP^{NP};
- Π_2^p: the class of decision problems whose complements are in Σ_2^p. This class is also denoted as $coNP^{NP}$;
- Δ_2^p: the class of decision problems which are solvable in polynomial time by deterministic Turing machines with an *NP* oracle. This class is also denoted as P^{NP};
- $\Delta_2^p[log(n)]$: the class of decision problems which are solvable in polynomial time by deterministic Turing machines with an *NP* oracle invoked $O(log(n))$ times. This class is also denoted as $P^{NP[log(n)]}$;

Chapter 3
Repairing and Querying: the Fundamental Decision Problems

Abstract In this chapter, we introduce some fundamental decision problems related to repairing and querying inconsistent data. Specifically, we formalize the *repair existence problem*, the *minimal repair checking problem*, and the *consistent query answer problem*, and analyze their computational complexity in the presence of databases inconsistent w.r.t. a given set of aggregate constraints. In this regard, we provide a thorough characterization, as we investigate the sensitivity of the computational complexity of these problems to several aspects: the domain of numerical attributes (integers or rationals), the form of the aggregate constraints considered (steady or not), and the minimality semantics (*card* or *set-minimal*).

3.1 Repair Existence Problem (RE)

The problem of deciding whether a database inconsistent w.r.t. a set of aggregate constraints can be repaired is defined as follows:

Definition 3.1 (REPAIR EXISTENCE (RE)). Let $\mathscr{D}$ be a fixed database scheme, and $\mathscr{AC}$ a fixed set of aggregate constraints on $\mathscr{D}$. RE is the problem of deciding whether a given instance of $\mathscr{D}$ belongs to the set

$$\{D \mid D \text{ is an instance of } \mathscr{D} \text{ and there exists a repair for } D \text{ w.r.t. } \mathscr{D} \text{ and } \mathscr{AC}\}$$

In the following, we denote with RE^{Δ} the version of the RE problem where every measure attribute in $\mathscr{M}_{\mathscr{D}}$ is associated with the domain Δ. Hence, $\text{RE}^{\mathbb{Z}}$ (resp., $\text{RE}^{\mathbb{Q}}$) is the version of the repair existence problem where all the measure attributes are constrained to range over the domain $\mathbb{Z}$ (resp., $\mathbb{Q}$) . An analogous notation will be used for the decision problems that will be defined later, i.e., the minimal repair checking (MRC) and consistent query answer (CQA) defined in Sections 3.2 and 3.3, respectively.

As a preliminary result, we have that, if at least one repair ρ exists for a database D w.r.t. a set of aggregate constraints $\mathscr{AC}$, then there is a repair ρ' for D w.r.t. $\mathscr{AC}$

which has polynomial size [1] and such that it updates a subset of the pairs $\langle$*tuple, attribute*$\rangle$ updated by ρ.

Lemma 3.1. *Let $\mathscr{D}$ be a database scheme, $\mathscr{AC}$ a set of aggregate constraints on $\mathscr{D}$, and D an instance of $\mathscr{D}$ such that D is not consistent w.r.t. $\mathscr{D}$ and $\mathscr{AC}$. If there is a repair ρ for D w.r.t. $\mathscr{D}$ and $\mathscr{AC}$, then there is a repair ρ' for D w.r.t. $\mathscr{D}$ and $\mathscr{AC}$ such that*

- $\lambda(\rho') \subseteq \lambda(\rho)$, *and*
- ρ' *has polynomial size w.r.t. D.*

Intuitively, the result of the lemma follows from the fact that we can define a system of linear inequality $In(\rho, D, \mathscr{D}, \mathscr{AC})$ such that given a repair ρ for D w.r.t. $\mathscr{D}$ and $\mathscr{AC}$, ρ corresponds to a solution $\hat{x}(\rho)$ of $In(\rho, D, \mathscr{D}, \mathscr{AC})$. Basically, each variable of $In(\rho, D, \mathscr{D}, \mathscr{AC})$ corresponds to a pair $\langle$*tuple, attribute*$\rangle$ changed by ρ, and the inequalities appropriately encode all the constraints of $\mathscr{AC}$ violated by D and the domain constraints. It is worth noting that $In(\rho, D, \mathscr{D}, \mathscr{AC})$ must be defined so that any other solution $\hat{x}'$ of $In(\rho, D, \mathscr{D}, \mathscr{AC})$ still corresponds to a repair ρ'. This is not trivial since it must be the case that assigning the values of $\hat{x}'$ to the corresponding pairs $\langle$*tuple, attribute*$\rangle$ of D the following hold: (i) D is consistent w.r.t. the set of aggregate constraints $\mathscr{AC}$ originally violated by D, and (ii) no violations of constraints in $\mathscr{AC}$ possibly not encoded in $In(\rho, D, \mathscr{D}, \mathscr{AC})$ are triggered. As the size of $In(\rho, D, \mathscr{D}, \mathscr{AC})$ is polynomial w.r.t. the size of D and since every feasible system of linear inequalities admits a polynomial bounded solution, the result of the lemma follow. The detailed proof of Lemma 3.1, as well as those of the theorems stated in this chapter, can be found in [26].

The result Lemma 3.1 entails that the repair existence problem is in *NP*, since when deciding the existence of a repair for an inconsistent we can limit the search space to polynomial size sets of updates. The following theorem provides a tight characterization of the complexity of RE.

Theorem 3.1. RE$^{\Delta}$ *with $\Delta \in \{\mathbb{Z}, \mathbb{Q}\}$ is NP-complete.*

We will see in Section 2.4 that the repair existence problem become tractable in the case that the aggregate constraints are steady and measure attributes range over the domain of rationals.

3.2 Minimal Repair Checking Problem (MRC)

We now address the characterization of the problem of deciding whether a given repair is minimal, under either the *card-* or the *set-* minimal semantics.

The minimal repair checking is defined as follows.

---

[1] The size of an atomic update $u = \langle t, A, v \rangle$ is determined by the size of the representation of the (integer or rational) number v. In turn, the size of a set U of atomic updates is given by sum of the sizes of the atomic updates in U.

Definition 3.2 (MINIMAL REPAIR CHECKING (MRC)). Let $\mathscr{D}$ be a fixed database scheme and $\mathscr{A}\mathscr{C}$ a fixed set of aggregate constraints on $\mathscr{D}$. Given an instance D of $\mathscr{D}$, and a repair ρ for D w.r.t. $\mathscr{D}$ and $\mathscr{A}\mathscr{C}$, MRC$_{\mathscr{S}}$ (with $\mathscr{S} \in \{card, set\}$) is the problem of deciding whether (D, ρ) belongs to the set

$$\{(D', \rho') \mid D' \text{ is an instance of } \mathscr{D} \text{ and } \rho' \text{ is an } \mathscr{S}\text{-minimal repair for } D' \\ \text{w.r.t. } \mathscr{D} \text{ and } \mathscr{A}\mathscr{C}\}$$

The following theorem characterizes the complexity of the MRC problem.

Theorem 3.2. MRC$_{\mathscr{S}}^{\Delta}$ with $\Delta \in \{\mathbb{Z}, \mathbb{Q}\}$ and $\mathscr{S} \in \{card, set\}$ in coNP-complete.

Hence the computational complexity of the problem of deciding whether a given repair is minimal does not depend neither on the domain of measure attributes, nor on the semantics adopted. Interesting enough, we will see in Section 2.4 that the MRC$_{set}^{\mathbb{Q}}$ problem becomes tractable in the presence of steady aggregate constraints.

3.3 Consistent Query Answer Problem (CQA)

We now define consistent query answer problem and characterize its complexity. We recall that $q_{\mathscr{D}, \mathscr{A}\mathscr{C}}^{\mathscr{S}}(D)$ denotes the consistent answer of the query q posed on the database D, instance of $\mathscr{D}$, in the presence of the set of aggregate constraints $\mathscr{A}\mathscr{C}$ (see Definition 2.8)

Definition 3.3 (CONSISTENT QUERY ANSWER PROBLEM (CQA)). Let $\mathscr{D}$ be a fixed database scheme, $\mathscr{A}\mathscr{C}$ a fixed set of aggregate constraints on $\mathscr{D}$, and q a fixed query over $\mathscr{D}$. CQA$_{\mathscr{S}}$, with $\mathscr{S} \in \{set, card\}$, is the problem of deciding whether a given instance of $\mathscr{D}$ belongs to the set

$$\{D \mid D \text{ is an instance of } \mathscr{D} \text{ and } q_{\mathscr{D}, \mathscr{A}\mathscr{C}}^{\mathscr{S}}(D) \text{ is true }\}.$$

Before providing the complexity characterization of the CQA problem, we introduce a new lemma extending the result of Lemma 3.1. Basically, the following lemma states that, if a database D admits a repair ρ such that a given query q is true (resp., false) on $\rho(D)$, then there is a polynomial-size repair ρ' for D such that q is true (resp., false) on $\rho'(D)$.

Lemma 3.2. Let $\mathscr{D}$ be a database scheme, $\mathscr{A}\mathscr{C}$ a set of aggregate constraints on $\mathscr{D}$, D an instance of $\mathscr{D}$ and $q = R(a_1, \ldots, a_n)$ a query over $\mathscr{D}$. If there is a repair ρ for D w.r.t. $\mathscr{D}$ and $\mathscr{A}\mathscr{C}$ such that $q \in \rho(D)$ (resp. $q \notin \rho(D)$), then there is a repair ρ' for D w.r.t. $\mathscr{D}$ and $\mathscr{A}\mathscr{C}$ such that:

(i) $\lambda(\rho') \subseteq \lambda(\rho)$,
(ii) $q \in \rho'(D)$ (resp. $q \notin \rho'(D)$), and
(iii) ρ' has polynomial size w.r.t. D and q.

The main consequence of this lemma regards minimal repairs. That is, the existence of an $\mathscr{S}$-minimal repair ρ (with $\mathscr{S} \in \{card, set\}$) such that q is true (resp., false) on $\rho(D)$ implies the existence of a polynomial-size $\mathscr{S}$-minimal repair ρ' such that q is true (resp., false) on $\rho'(D)$. This will allow us to restrict the search space of minimal repairs making a query either true or false to polynomial-size repairs. Intuitively enough, this property can be exploited to provide an upper bound on the complexity of the CQA problem for both the *set*- and *card*-minimal semantics.

A tight characterization of the complexity of the CQA problem is provided by the following theorem.

Theorem 3.3. CQA_{set}^{Δ} *is* Π_2^p-*complete, whereas* CQA_{card}^{Δ} *is* $\Delta_2^p[\log n]$-*complete, where* $\Delta \in \{\mathbb{Z}, \mathbb{Q}\}$

In order to provide tight lower bounds on the complexity of CQA, the analogy between CQA and the implication problem in belief revision [32] is exploited. The implication problem is that of deciding whether a formula is true according to the revised theory resulting from applying a revision formula on a given theory. Basically, the application of a revision formula on a theory results in revising the beliefs by taking into account more precise or reliable information on the real world. Specifically, different revision operators can be exploited to revise a given knowledge base, each of them corresponding to a different semantics ensuring that as much information as possible is preserved. For our *set*- and *card*-minimal semantics, we rely on the revision operators introduced by Satoh and Dalal, respectively. The analogy between the implication problem of IP and CQA is that the knowledge base and the revision formula of IP can be viewed as a database and a set of constraints of CQA, respectively. Technically, the main difference is that in the formulation of IP, the revision formula is part of the input, while in our formulation of CQA aggregate constraints are fixed. To prove Theorem 3.3, we defined reductions where both the knowledge base and the revision formula of an IP instance are translated into the database D of a CQA instance, where appropriate aggregate constraints of fixed size are defined.

3.4 RE, MRC and CQA under Steady Aggregate Constraints

In this section, we characterize the complexity of the decision problems introduced in the previous sections in the case that the aggregate constraints considered are steady. We will denote as STEADY-RE$^{\Delta}$ (resp., STEADY-MRC$^{\Delta}$, STEADY-CQA$^{\Delta}$), with $\Delta \in \{\mathbb{Z}, \mathbb{Q}\}$, the problem RE$^{\Delta}$ (resp., MRC$^{\Delta}$, CQA$^{\Delta}$) in the case that aggregate constraints are steady. Interestingly, we will show that the "steadiness" of constraints makes the complexity of some of these problems become sensitive to the domain of measure attributes. In particular, the following theorem states that the complexity of the steady-version of these problems does not change w.r.t. the general case in the case of integer measure attributes.

Theorem 3.4. *The complexity of* STEADY-RE$^{\mathbb{Z}}$, STEADY-MRC$^{\mathbb{Z}}_{\mathscr{S}}$, *and* STEADY-CQA$^{\mathbb{Z}}_{\mathscr{S}}$ *with* $\mathscr{S} \in \{card, set\}$ *is the same as that of their non-steady versions.*

We now address the complexity characterization of STEADY-RE, STEADY-MRC$_{\mathscr{S}}$, and STEADY-CQA$_{\mathscr{S}}$ in the case of rational measure attributes. We show that the complexity of some of these problems decreases in the presence of rational measure attributes.

Rational-variant of Repair Existence

Differently from the case where the numerical domain is $\mathbb{Z}$, applying the steadiness restriction in the presence of rational measure attributes makes the repair existence problem tractable. Basically, this is due to two reasons. On the one hand, the fact that the aggregate constraints are steady makes it possible to translate STEADY-RE to the problem of deciding the feasibility of a system of linear inequalities. On the other hand, the fact that measure attributes are rational makes this system of inequalities contain rational variables only, which implies that its feasibility can be decided in polynomial time [33].

Theorem 3.5. STEADY-RE$^{\mathbb{Q}}$ *is P-complete.*

Rational-variant of Minimal-Repair Checking

The complexity of both STEADY-MRC$^{\mathbb{Q}}_{card}$ and STEADY-MRC$^{\mathbb{Q}}_{set}$ is characterized in the following theorem.

Theorem 3.6. STEADY-MRC$^{\mathbb{Q}}_{card}$ *is coNP-complete, whereas* STEADY-MRC$^{\mathbb{Q}}_{set}$ *is P-complete.*

Although STEADY-MRC$^{\mathbb{Q}}_{card}$ has the same tight lower bound as the corresponding more general problem MRC$^{\mathbb{Q}}_{card}$, moving from the *card-* to the *set*-minimal semantics entails a lowering of the complexity of STEADY-MRC in the presence of rational measure attributes, as STEADY-MRC$^{\mathbb{Q}}_{set}$ becomes tractable. Intuitively, the tractability of STEADY-MRC$^{\mathbb{Q}}_{set}$ follows from the fact that a repair ρ is not *set*-minimal iff updating at least one value less than ρ suffices to fix the inconsistency (that is, iff there is a repair ρ' such that $\lambda(\rho') \subset \lambda(\rho)$ and $|\lambda(\rho')| \leq |\lambda(\rho)| - 1$). Hence, the existence of such a repair ρ' can be decided by solving at most $|\lambda(\rho)|$ instances of STEADY-RE obtained from the instance of STEADY-MRC$^{\mathbb{Q}}_{set}$ by making unchangeable (through appropriate aggregate constraints) all the measure attributes of the database but $|\lambda(\rho)| - 1$ chosen among those updated by ρ. Since STEADY-RE is tractable (Theorem 3.5), it easy to see that the above-described strategy works in polynomial time.

Rational-variant of Consistent Query Answer

The following theorem show that the complexity of CQA under the *card*-minimal semantics is not lowered by the introduction of steady aggregate constraints, differently from the *set*-minimal semantics, as STEADY-CQA$_{set}^{Q}$ is shown to be *coNP*-complete.

Theorem 3.7. STEADY-CQA$_{card}^{Q}$ *is* $\Delta_2^p[log n]$-*complete, whereas* STEADY-CQA$_{set}^{Q}$ *is coNP-complete.*

Basically, the membership in coNP of STEADY-CQA$_{set}^{Q}$ derives from the fact that STEADY-MRC$_{set}^{Q}$ is in *P*.

3.5 Summary of the complexity results

A summary of the complexity results obtained so far is shown in Table 3.1, where all the problems are shown to be complete for the classes reported in the cells of the table.

Constraints $\mathscr{AC}$	Domain Δ	RE$^{\Delta}$	MRC$_{card}^{\Delta}$	CQA$_{card}^{\Delta}$	MRC$_{set}^{\Delta}$	CQA$_{set}^{\Delta}$
General	$\mathbb{Z}$	*NP*	*coNP*	$\Delta_2^p[log n]$	*coNP*	Π_2^p
	$\mathbb{Q}$	*NP*	*coNP*	$\Delta_2^p[log n]$	*coNP*	Π_2^p
Steady	$\mathbb{Z}$	*NP*	*coNP*	$\Delta_2^p[log n]$	*coNP*	Π_2^p
	$\mathbb{Q}$	*P*	*coNP*	$\Delta_2^p[log n]$	*P*	*coNP*

Table 3.1 Summary of complexity results

The results in the above-reported table show that the choice of the semantics (*card*- or *set*- minimality), the class of aggregate constraints (general or steady), as well as the domain of the numerical data involved in the constraints, introduce different sources of complexity. Specifically, in the presence of general aggregate constraints, the complexity of the analyzed problems does not depend on the domain of the numerical data, but only on the semantics. This does not hold in the presence of steady aggregate constraints. In fact, in this case, RE is *NP*-complete if the domain of the numerical data is $\mathbb{Z}$, whereas it is *P*-complete if the domain is $\mathbb{Q}$. Analogously, under the *set*-minimal semantics, MRC and CQA are *coNP*- and Π_2^p- complete, respectively, if the numerical data domain is $\mathbb{Z}$, and their complexity becomes *P*- and *coNP*- complete, respectively, if the numerical data domain is $\mathbb{Q}$.

It is worth noting that, under the *card*-minimal semantics, the complexity of MRC and CQA does not depend on the numerical data domain and the class of aggregate constraint considered. This does not hold under the *set*-minimal semantics.

Interestingly enough, while, in general, the complexity of CQA under the *set*-minimal semantics is higher than the case of *card*-minimal semantics, the CQA problem under *set*-minimal semantics becomes easier than the same problem under *card*-minimal semantics in the presence of steady aggregate constraints, if the numerical data are rationals. Moreover, for this class of constraints and this numerical domain, also the complexity of the MRC problem under *set*-minimal semantics becomes lower than that of the MRC problem under *card*-minimal semantics.

Chapter 4
Computing *Card*-minimal Repairs

Abstract In this chapter, we present a technique for computing *card*-minimal repairs in the presence of steady aggregate constraints. Thus, differently from the (decision) problems introduced in Chapter 3, we here address a search problem, which is relevant in practice as, in several applications, the availability of a consistent version of the data is mandatory for accomplishing a number of analysis tasks. We also show how this technique can be extended to deal with *weak* aggregate constraints, i.e., constraints defining conditions that are expected (but not due) to be satisfied, which usually encode common belief or gossip about the world represented by the data. Specifically, the search of the repair is refined by trying to satisfy all the given (strong) aggregate constraints and to maximize the number of weak constraints satisfied. This way, the search is driven towards *preferred repairs*, i.e., repairs which can be assumed to be "more reasonable", compared with repairs satisfying the (strong) aggregate constraints only.

4.1 Searching for Reasonable Repairs

The problem of computing (minimal) repairs of inconsistent numerical data is relevant in several applications, since the availability of a consistent version of the data is mandatory for accomplishing a number of analysis tasks. For instance, in our running example, in order to perform analysis aiming at determining liquidity problems as well as the financial reliability of a company, a consistent version of the balance-sheets of the company should be available.

In this chapter we address the problem of computing reasonable repairs for database violating aggregate constraints. Specifically, we first present a technique for computing *card*-minimal repairs in the presence of steady aggregate constraints. Then, we extend the proposed technique to work in a more general setting, where well-established information on the application domain of data to be repaired are exploited to choose the most reasonable repairs (namely, *preferred* repairs) among the *card*-minimal ones.

S. Flesca et al., *Repairing and Querying Databases under Aggregate Constraints*,
SpringerBriefs in Computer Science, DOI 10.1007/978-1-4614-1641-8_4, © The Author(s) 2011

We will show that both the problems of finding a *card*-minimal repair and a *preferred* repair for a database D w.r.t. a set of steady aggregate constraints $\mathscr{A}\mathscr{C}$ can be modeled as a MILP [1] (Mixed Integer Linear Programming) problem [33], thus allowing us to adopt standard techniques addressing MILP problems to accomplish the computation of reasonable repairs. We point out that translating the problem of finding a *card*-minimal repair (as well as that of finding a preferred repair) into an MILP problem (which is *NP*-hard) is reasonable, since the search problem we are considering is *NP*-hard too. This easily follows from the fact that there is a straightforward reduction to this problem from the *coNP*-hard problem STEADY-MRC$_{card}$, the steady version of the *card*-minimal repair checking problem studied in Chapter 3. In fact, an instance of STEADY-MRC$_{card}$ can be solved by computing a *card*-minimal repair for the given database w.r.t. the given set of steady aggregate constraints, and then comparing its cardinality with that of the repair whose *card*-minimality has to be checked.

Our technique for computing *card*-minimal repairs is introduced in the next two sections. First, we explain how aggregate constraints can be translated into sets of inequalities (Section 4.2). Then, we show how this translation can be used to define a MILP instance which computes the *card*-minimal repairs (Section 4.3). Later, in Sections 4.4 and 4.5, we will formalize the concept of *preferred* repairs, and extend our technique for computing *card*-minimal repairs to deal with this kind of repairs.

4.2 Expressing Steady Aggregate Constraints as Sets of Inequalities

In the following we assume that a database scheme $\mathscr{D}$, an instance D of $\mathscr{D}$, and a set of steady aggregate constraints $\mathscr{A}\mathscr{C}$ on $\mathscr{D}$ are given. We show how the triplet $\langle \mathscr{D}, \mathscr{A}\mathscr{C}, D \rangle$ can be translated into a set of linear inequalities $\mathscr{S}(\mathscr{D}, \mathscr{A}\mathscr{C}, D)$ such that every solution of $\mathscr{S}(\mathscr{D}, \mathscr{A}\mathscr{C}, D)$ corresponds to a (possibly not-minimal) repair for D w.r.t. $\mathscr{A}\mathscr{C}$.

We first describe the translation for a single steady aggregate constraint ac having the following form:

$$\forall \mathbf{x} \left(\phi(\mathbf{x}) \implies \sum_{i=1}^{n} c_i \cdot \chi_i(\mathbf{y}_i) \leq K \right)$$

where $\forall i \in [1..n]$, the aggregation function $\chi_i(\mathbf{y})$ has the form $\langle R_i, e_i, \alpha_i(\mathbf{y}_i) \rangle$. The translation results from the three steps described in what follow. We assume that, for every relation scheme R_ℓ in $\mathscr{D}$, its instance in D is r_ℓ.

---

[1] If the domain of numerical attributes is restricted to $\mathbb{Z}$, then it can be formulated as an ILP problem.

1) *Associating variables with pairs* ⟨tuple, measure attribute⟩*:*
For each tuple t of a relation instance r_ℓ in D and measure attribute $A_j \in \mathcal{M}_{R_\ell}$, we create the integer variable z_{t,A_j} whose domain is the same as A_j ;

2) *Translating each aggregation function* χ_i *into sums of variables and constants:*
Let $\Theta(ac)$ be the set of the ground substitutions of variables in **x** with constants such that $\forall \theta \in \Theta(ac)$ $\phi(\theta\mathbf{x})$ is *true* on D. For every ground substitution $\theta \in \Theta(ac)$ and every χ_i, we denote as $T_{\chi_i}(\theta)$ the set of tuples involved in the evaluation of χ_i w.r.t. θ, that is $T_{\chi_i}(\theta) = \{t : t \in r_i \wedge t \models \alpha_i(\theta\mathbf{y_i})\}$, where r_i is the instance in D of the relation scheme R_i in χ_i.
Then, for every ground substitution $\theta \in \Theta(ac)$, we define the translation of χ_i w.r.t. θ as:

$$\mathscr{P}(\chi_i, \theta) = \begin{cases} \sum_{t \in T_{\chi_i}(\theta)} z_{t,A_j} & \text{if } e_i \text{ is the measure attribute } A_j; \\ \\ \sum_{t \in T_{\chi_i}(\theta)} e_i(t) & \text{otherwise.} \end{cases}$$

3) *Translating the steady aggregate constraint ac into a set of linear inequalities:*
The constraint ac is translated into the set $\mathscr{S}(\mathscr{D}, ac, D)$ of linear inequalities containing an inequality for every ground substitution in $\Theta(ac)$, that is

$$\mathscr{S}(\mathscr{D}, ac, D) = \bigcup_{\theta \in \Theta(ac)} \{\sum_{i=1}^{n} c_i \cdot \mathscr{P}(\chi_i, \theta) \le K\}$$

Finally, the system of linear inequalities $\mathscr{S}(\mathscr{D}, \mathscr{AC}, D)$, which takes into account all the aggregate constraints in $\mathscr{AC}$, is then defined as

$$\mathscr{S}(\mathscr{D}, \mathscr{AC}, D) = \bigcup_{ac \in \mathscr{AC}} \mathscr{S}(\mathscr{D}, ac, D)$$

For the sake of simplicity, in the following we assume that the pairs $\langle t, A_j \rangle$, where A_j is the name of a measure attribute of tuple t, are associated with distinct integer indexes. The set of these indexes will be denoted as $\mathscr{I}$. Therefore, being i the integer associated with the pair $\langle t, A_j \rangle$, the variable z_{t,A_j} will be denoted as z_i.

Example 4.1. In "Balance Sheets" example, we associate each pair $\langle t_i, Value \rangle$ with the integer i, thus $\mathscr{I} = \{1, \ldots, 20\}$. The translation of the (steady) aggregate constraints $\kappa_1, \kappa_2, \kappa_3$, introduced in Example 1.3 (and formalized in Examples 2.2 and 2.3), is as follows (we explicitly write equalities instead of inequalities):

$$\kappa_1 \begin{cases} z_2 + z_3 = z_4 \\ z_5 + z_6 + z_7 = z_8 \\ z_{12} + z_{13} = z_{14} \\ z_{15} + z_{16} + z_{17} = z_{18} \end{cases} \qquad \kappa_2 \begin{cases} z_4 - z_8 = z_9 \\ z_{14} - z_{18} = z_{19} \end{cases} \qquad \kappa_3 \begin{cases} z_1 - z_9 = z_{10} \\ z_{11} - z_{19} = z_{20} \end{cases}$$

The set of inequalities $\mathscr{S}(\mathscr{D}, \mathscr{AC}, D)$ consists of all the inequalities above.

There is a one-to-one correspondence between every solution s of $\mathscr{S}(\mathscr{D}, \mathscr{AC}, D)$ and a repair $\rho(s)$ for D w.r.t. $\mathscr{D}$ and $\mathscr{AC}$. In particular, the solution s corresponding to a repair $\rho(s)$ assigns to each z_i the value taken by $t[A_j]$ in the database $\rho(D)$, where $\langle t, A_j \rangle$ is the pair *tuple, attribute* associated with z_i. This correspondence may not hold if the set of aggregate constraints $\mathscr{AC}$ is not steady, since performing on D updates corresponding to a solution of $\mathscr{S}(\mathscr{D}, \mathscr{AC}, D)$ may trigger violations of constraints which were not encoded in $\mathscr{S}(\mathscr{D}, \mathscr{AC}, D)$. Our technique exploits the restrictions imposed on steady aggregate constraints w.r.t. general aggregate constraints to accomplish the computation of a repair. As explained above, this approach does not work for (general) aggregate constraints.

Example 4.2. Consider the solution of $\mathscr{S}(\mathscr{D}, \mathscr{AC}, D)$ which assigns to each z_i the value $t_i[Value]$, except for z_2, z_3, z_{18}, which are assigned 1000, 250, and 1190, respectively. This solution corresponds to the non-minimal repair ρ_2 of Example 2.10.
$\square$

4.3 Computing Minimal Repairs

Our approach for computing card-minimal repairs is based on the resolution of specific MILP problems, defined starting from the MILP problem introduced below.

Definition 4.1 (*MILP*($\mathscr{D}, \mathscr{AC}, D$)). Given a database scheme $\mathscr{D}$, a set $\mathscr{AC}$ of steady aggregate constraints on $\mathscr{D}$, and an instance D of $\mathscr{D}$, *MILP*($\mathscr{D}, \mathscr{AC}, D$) is a MILP of the form:

$$
\begin{cases}
\mathbf{A} \times \mathbf{z} \leq \mathbf{B} & \\
w_i = z_i - v_i & \forall i \in \mathscr{I} \\
w_i - M\delta_i \leq 0 & \forall i \in \mathscr{I} \\
-w_i - M\delta_i \leq 0 & \forall i \in \mathscr{I} \\
z_i - M \leq 0 & \forall i \in \mathscr{I} \\
-z_i - M \leq 0 & \forall i \in \mathscr{I} \\
z_i, w_i \in \mathbb{Q} & \forall i \in \mathscr{I}_{\mathbb{Q}} \\
z_i, w_i \in \mathbb{Z} & \forall i \in \mathscr{I}_{\mathbb{Z}} \\
\delta_i \in \{0, 1\} & \forall i \in \mathscr{I}
\end{cases}
$$

where:
(i) $\mathbf{A} \times \mathbf{z} \leq \mathbf{B}$ is the set of inequalities $\mathscr{S}(\mathscr{D}, \mathscr{AC}, D)$ ($\mathbf{z}$ is the vector of variables z_i with $i \in \mathscr{I}$);
(ii) for each $i \in \mathscr{I}$, v_i is the database value corresponding to the variable z_i, that is, if z_i is associated with the pair $\langle t, A_j \rangle$, then $v_i = t[A_j]$;
(iii) $M = n \cdot (ma)^{2m+1}$, where: a is the maximum among the modules of the coefficients in $\mathbf{A}$ and of the values v_i, and $m = |\mathscr{I}| + r$, and $n = 2 \cdot |\mathscr{I}| + r$, where r is the number of rows of $\mathbf{A}$.
(iv) $\mathscr{I}_{\mathbb{Q}} \subseteq \mathscr{I}$ (resp., $\mathscr{I}_{\mathbb{Z}} \subseteq \mathscr{I}$) is the set of the indexes of the variables z_i and w_i defined on the domain $\mathbb{Q}$ (resp., $\mathbb{Z}$).

Basically, for every solution of *MILP*($\mathscr{D}, \mathscr{AC}, D$), the variables z_i are assigned values which satisfy $\mathbf{A} \times \mathbf{z} \leq \mathbf{B}$ (that is, $\mathscr{S}(\mathscr{D}, \mathscr{AC}, D)$). Hence, the variables z_i of a solution of $MILP(\mathcal{D}, \mathcal{AC}, D)$ take values which, once assigned to the corresponding pairs *tuple, attribute*, make the database satisfy the aggregate constraints $\mathcal{AC}$.

In the definition above, each variable w_i represents the difference between the variable z_i associated with a pair $\langle t, A_j \rangle$ and the original database value $v_i = t[A_j]$. The constant M is introduced for a twofold objective: considering solutions of the first two inequalities with polynomial size[2] w.r.t. the database size, and building a mechanism for counting the number of variables z_i which are assigned a value different from the original value of the corresponding pair *tuple, attribute*. The value of M derives from a well-known general result shown in [44] regarding the existence of bounded solutions of systems of linear equalities. In our case, this result implies that, if the first two (in)equalities of $MILP(\mathcal{D}, \mathcal{AC}, D)$ have at least one solution, then they admit at least one solution where (absolute) values are less than M. Hence, the inequalities of $MILP(\mathcal{D}, \mathcal{AC}, D)$ where M occurs entail that:

– $MILP(\mathcal{D}, \mathcal{AC}, D)$ has solution iff the first two inequalities have a solution. In particular, each solution of $MILP(\mathcal{D}, \mathcal{AC}, D)$ can be obtained by taking any solution of the first two inequalities with values less than M and then properly adjusting each δ_i;
– every solution of $MILP(\mathcal{D}, \mathcal{AC}, D)$ is of polynomial size w.r.t. the size of the database. In fact, solutions of the first two inequalities with values larger than M do not correspond to solutions of $MILP(\mathcal{D}, \mathcal{AC}, D)$, as, if $|w_i| > M$, there is no way of choosing δ_i to satisfy both $w_i - M\delta_i \leq 0$ and $-w_i - M\delta_i \leq 0$.
– for every solution of $MILP(\mathcal{D}, \mathcal{AC}, D)$, the sum of the values assigned to variables δ_i is an upper bound on the number of variables z_i different from the corresponding v_i. In fact, if w_i has a value different from 0 (meaning that z_i has a value different from the "original" v_i) then δ_i is assigned 1. It is easy to see that the vice versa does not hold, thus this sum does not represent the exact number of variables z_i different from the original values.

For any solution s of $MILP(\mathcal{D}, \mathcal{AC}, D)$, the value taken by variable z in s will be denoted as $s[z]$. The above-mentioned properties of $MILP(\mathcal{D}, \mathcal{AC}, D)$ are stated in the theorem below.

Theorem 4.1. *Every solution s of an instance of $MILP(\mathcal{D}, \mathcal{AC}, D)$ one-to-one corresponds to a repair $\rho(s)$ for D such that:*

(i) for each z_i associated with the pair $\langle t, A_j \rangle$ and such that $s[z_i] \neq t[A_j]$, $\rho(s)$ contains the atomic update $\langle t, A_i, s[z_i] \rangle$;
(ii) $\forall i \in \mathcal{I}$, it is the case that $-M \leq s[z_i] \leq M$;
(iii) $|\rho(s)| \leq \sum_{i \in \mathcal{I}} s[\delta_i]$.

Hence, the repair $\rho(s)$ defined by solution s of $MILP(\mathcal{D}, \mathcal{AC}, D)$ is such that its cardinality is bounded by $\sum_{i \in \mathcal{I}} \delta_i$ and its atomic updates assign values bounded by M. *Card*-minimal repairs can be evaluated by exploiting the following optimization problem.

---

[2] The size of M is polynomial in the size of the database, as it is bounded by $\log n + (2 \cdot m + 1) \cdot \log(ma)$.

Definition 4.2. Let $\mathscr{D}$ be a database scheme, $\mathscr{AC}$ a set of steady aggregate constraints on $\mathscr{D}$, and D an instance of $\mathscr{D}$.

$$OPT(\mathscr{D},\mathscr{AC},D) := \begin{array}{l} minimize \ \sum_{i\in\mathscr{I}} \delta_i \\ subject \ to \ MILP(\mathscr{D},\mathscr{AC},D) \end{array}$$

Lemma 3.1 (which ensures that if a repair exists for D w.r.t. $\mathscr{D}$ and $\mathscr{AC}$, then there is a *card*-minimal repair for D which is M-bounded) and Theorem 4.1 entails the following corollary, which provide a strategy for computing *card*-minimal repairs.

Corollary 4.1. *A repair for D w.r.t. $\mathscr{D}$ and $\mathscr{AC}$ exists iff $MILP(\mathscr{D},\mathscr{AC},D)$ has at least one solution. Moreover, the optimal value of $OPT(\mathscr{D},\mathscr{AC},D)$ coincides with the cardinality of any* card*-minimal repair for D w.r.t. $\mathscr{AC}$, and every solution s of $OPT(\mathscr{D},\mathscr{AC},D)$ define an M-bounded* card*-minimal repair $\rho(s)$ for D w.r.t. $\mathscr{AC}$.*

Example 4.3. The optimization problem $OPT(\mathscr{D},\mathscr{AC},D)$ obtained for "Balance Sheet" example is shown in Fig. 4.1, where we assume that the domain of attribute *Value* is $\mathbb{Z}$ (hence $I_\mathbb{Z} = \{1,\ldots,20\}$ and $I_\mathbb{R} = \emptyset$).

$$\min \sum_{i=1}^{20} \delta_i$$

$$\left\{ \begin{array}{ll}
z_2 + z_3 = z_4 & w_{11} = z_{11} - 80 \\
z_5 + z_6 + z_7 = z_8 & w_{12} = z_{12} - 1110 \\
z_{12} + z_{13} = z_{14} & w_{13} = z_{13} - 90 \\
z_{15} + z_{16} + z_{17} = z_{18} & w_{14} = z_{14} - 1200 \\
z_4 - z_8 = z_9 & w_{15} = z_{15} - 1130 \\
z_{14} - z_{18} = z_{19} & w_{16} = z_{16} - 40 \\
z_1 - z_9 = z_{10} & w_{17} = z_{17} - 20 \\
z_{11} - z_{19} = z_{20} & w_{18} = z_{18} - 1120 \\
w_1 = z_1 - 50 & w_{19} = z_{19} - 10 \\
w_2 = z_2 - 900 & w_{20} = z_{20} - 90 \\
w_3 = z_3 - 100 & w_i - M\delta_i \leq 0 \quad \forall i \in [1..20] \\
w_4 = z_4 - 1250 & -w_i - M\delta_i \leq 0 \quad \forall i \in [1..20] \\
w_5 = z_5 - 1120 & z_i - M \leq 0 \quad \forall i \in [1..20] \\
w_6 = z_6 - 20 & -z_i - M \leq 0 \quad \forall i \in [1..20] \\
w_7 = z_7 - 80 & z_i, w_i \in \mathbb{Z} \quad \forall i \in [1..20] \\
w_8 = z_8 - 1220 & \delta_i \in \{0,1\} \quad \forall i \in [1..20] \\
w_9 = z_9 - 30 & \\
w_{10} = z_{10} - 80 &
\end{array} \right.$$

Fig. 4.1 Instance of $OPT(\mathscr{D},\mathscr{AC},D)$ obtained for "Balance Sheet" example

This problem admits two optimal solutions, where the value of the objective function is equal to 2. In the first solution, δ_2 and δ_{18} are equal to 1, whereas the other δ_i are assigned 0. Moreover, the value of each variable $w_1,\ldots,w_{20}$ is 0 except for w_2 and w_{18} which are assigned 250 and 60, respectively. In the other solution, the variables δ_i assigned a value different from 0 are δ_3 and δ_{18}, and variable w_i are assigned 0 except for $w_3 = 250$ and $w_{18} = 60$. The *card*-minimal repairs corresponding to these solutions are $\rho_1 = \{ \langle t_2, Value, 1150 \rangle, \langle t_{18}, Value, 1190 \rangle \}$ and $\rho_5 = \{ \langle t_3, Value, 350 \rangle, \langle t_{18}, Value, 1190 \rangle \}$ of Example 2.12.   □

4.4 Preferred Repairs

In general, there may be several *card*-minimal repairs for a database violating a given set of aggregate constraints. For instance, in the "Balance Sheet" example, it is possible to repair the data by increasing the values of attribute *Value* in tuples t_2 and t_{18} up to 1150 and 1190, respectively (this strategy is that adopted by the *card*-minimal repair ρ_1). An alternative *card*-minimal repair consists of increasing the values of attribute *Value* in tuples t_3 and t_{18} up to 350 and 1190, respectively, (this strategy is that adopted by the *card*-minimal repair ρ_5). It would be important to exploit well-established information on the data to be repaired in order to choose the most reasonable repairs among those having minimum cardinality, hence ranking *card*-minimal repairs. For instance, in our running example, historical data retrieved from balance-sheets of past years could be exploited to find conditions which are likely to hold for the current-year balance-sheet, so that *card*-minimal repairs could be ordered according to the number of these conditions which are satisfied in the repaired database. As a matter of fact, consider our running example in the case that, for all the years preceding 2008, the value of *cash sales* was never less than 1000 and the value of *receivables* was never greater than 200. Then, the value of *cash sales* for the current year is not likely to be less than 1000, and the value of *receivables* is not likely to be greater than 200. These likely conditions can be interpreted as *weak constraints*, in the sense that their satisfaction is not mandatory. Weak constraints can be exploited for defining a repairing technique where inconsistent data are fixed in the "most likely" way. Specifically, the most likely ways of repairing inconsistent data are those corresponding to *card*-minimal repairs satisfying as many weak constraints as possible. For instance, if we consider the above-mentioned weak constraints in our running example, the *card*-minimal repair ρ_1 can be reasonably preferred to ρ_5, since the former yields a database which satisfies both the weak constraints.

Weak aggregate constraints are aggregate constraints with a "weak" semantics: in contrast with the traditional "strong" semantics of aggregate constraints (according to which the repaired data *must* satisfy all the conditions expressed), weak aggregate constraints express conditions which reasonably hold in the actual data, although satisfying them is not mandatory.

Example 4.4. The two conditions defined above (that is, "*it is likely that cash sales are greater than or equal to 1000*", and "*it is likely that receivables are less than or equal to 200*") can be expressed by the following weak aggregate constraints:

$$\omega_1: \quad BalanceSheets(x,\_,\_,\_,\_) \implies \quad \chi_2(x, \text{'cash sales'}) \geq 1000$$

$$\omega_2: \quad BalanceSheets(x,\_,\_,\_,\_) \implies \quad \chi_2(x, \text{'receivables'}) \leq 200$$

where χ_2 is the aggregation function defined in Example 2.1. $\square$

Intuitively, a *card*-minimal repair satisfying n_1 weak constraints is preferred to any other *card*-minimal repair satisfying $n_2 < n_1$ weak constraints.

We exploit this ordering criterion implied by weak constraints on the set of *card*-minimal repairs to define *preferred (card-minimal) repairs*, i.e., *card*-minimal repairs which are the most "reasonable" ones, in the sense that they satisfy as many weak aggregate constraints as possible.

Let $\mathcal{D}$ be a database scheme, D an instance of $\mathcal{D}$, and ω a weak aggregate constraint on $\mathcal{D}$ having the following form (see Definition 2.1):

$$\forall \mathbf{x} \left(\phi(\mathbf{x}) \implies \sum_{i=1}^{n} c_i \cdot \chi_i(\mathbf{y}_i) \leq K \right)$$

We denote the set of *ground weak constraints* obtained from the instantiation of ω on D as $gr(\omega, D)$. More formally, let $\Theta(\omega)$ be the set of the ground substitutions of variables in $\mathbf{x}$ with constants such that $\forall \theta \in \Theta(\omega) \ \phi(\theta \mathbf{x})$ is *true* on D, set of ground weak constraints is

$$gr(\omega, D) = \{\theta(\omega) \mid \theta \in \Theta(\omega)\}$$

Given a set of weak constraints $\mathcal{W}$ on $\mathcal{D}$, we denote as $gr(\mathcal{W}, D)$ the set of ground weak constraints obtained from the instantiation of every $\omega \in \mathcal{W}$ on D, i.e.,

$$gr(\mathcal{W}, D) = \bigcup_{\omega \in \mathcal{W}} \{gr(\omega, D)\}$$

Let ρ be a *card*-minimal repair for D w.r.t. a set of aggregate constraints $\mathcal{AC}$ on $\mathcal{D}$, and $\mathcal{W}$ be a set of weak constraints on $\mathcal{D}$. We will denote as $\gamma(\rho, \mathcal{W}, D)$ the number of ground weak constraints in $gr(\mathcal{W}, \rho(D))$ which are not satisfied.

Definition 4.3 (Preferred repair). Let $\mathcal{D}$ be a database scheme, $\mathcal{AC}$ a set of aggregate constraints on $\mathcal{D}$, $\mathcal{W}$ a set of weak aggregate constraints on $\mathcal{D}$, and D an instance of $\mathcal{D}$. A *card*-minimal repair ρ for D w.r.t. $\mathcal{D}$ and $\mathcal{AC}$ is said to be a *preferred repair* for D w.r.t. $\mathcal{AC}$ and $\mathcal{W}$ iff there is no *card*-minimal repair ρ' for D w.r.t. $\mathcal{D}$ and $\mathcal{AC}$ such that $\gamma(\rho', \mathcal{W}, D) < \gamma(\rho, \mathcal{W}, D)$.

Example 4.5. As explained in Example 2.12, in our running example the set of *card*-minimal repairs is

$$\rho_{\mathcal{D}, \mathcal{AC}}^{card}(D) = \{ \ \rho_1 = \{ \langle t_2, Value, 1150 \rangle, \langle t_{18}, Value, 1190 \rangle \}$$
$$\rho_5 = \{ \langle t_3, Value, 350 \rangle, \langle t_{18}, Value, 1190 \rangle \}\}$$

Let $\mathcal{W} = \{\omega_1, \omega_2\}$ be the set of weak constraints introduced in Example 4.4. The set $gr(\mathcal{W}, \rho_1(D))$ of ground weak aggregate constraints on the database repaired by

ρ_1 is the following:

$$\omega_1^a : BalanceSheets(2008, Receipts, cash\ sales, det, 1150) \implies$$
$$\chi_2(2008, \text{'cash sales'}) \geq 1000$$

$$\omega_1^b : BalanceSheets(2009, Receipts, cash\ sales, det, 1110) \implies$$
$$\chi_2(2009, \text{'cash sales'}) \geq 1000$$

$$\omega_2^a : BalanceSheets(2008, Receipts, receivables, det, 100) \implies$$
$$\chi_2(2008, receivables') \leq 200$$

$$\omega_2^b : BalanceSheets(2009, Receipts, receivables, det, 90) \implies$$
$$\chi_2(2009, receivables') \leq 200$$

The set $gr(\mathcal{W}, \rho_5(D))$ of ground weak aggregate constraints on the database repaired by ρ_5 is as follows:

$$\omega_1^c : BalanceSheets(2008, Receipts, cash\ sales, det, 900) \implies$$
$$\chi_2(2008, \text{'cash sales'}) \geq 1000$$

$$\omega_1^d : BalanceSheets(2009, Receipts, cash\ sales, det, 1110) \implies$$
$$\chi_2(2009, \text{'cash sales'}) \geq 1000$$

$$\omega_2^c : BalanceSheets(2008, Receipts, receivables, det, 350) \implies$$
$$\chi_2(2008, receivables') \leq 200$$

$$\omega_2^d : BalanceSheets(2009, Receipts, receivables, det, 90) \implies$$
$$\chi_2(2009, receivables') \leq 200$$

It is easy to see that all of the ground instantiations of ω_2 are satisfied by both $\rho_1(D)$ and $\rho_5(D)$. Moreover, $\rho_1(D)$ also satisfies both of the instantiations of ω_1, whereas $\rho_5(D)$ satisfies only one instantiation of ω_1 (namely, ω_1^d). Hence, $\gamma(\rho_1, \mathcal{W}, D) = 0$, since $\rho_1(D)$ satisfies all of the ground aggregate constraints derived from ω_1 and ω_2, and $\gamma(\rho_5, \mathcal{W}, D) = 1$, since $\rho_5(D)$ violates the ground aggregate constraints ω_1^c. Thus, ρ_1 is a preferred repair w.r.t. $\mathcal{AC}$ and $\mathcal{W}$. $\square$

4.5 Computing Preferred Repairs

Before tackling the problem of computing preferred *card*-minimal repairs, we investigate some issues related to the existence of preferred repairs from a theoretical standpoint. The following theorem extends some of the results presented in Chapther 3 to the case of preferred repairs.

Theorem 4.2. *Let $\mathscr{D}$ be a database scheme, $\mathscr{AC}$ a set of aggregate constraints on $\mathscr{D}$, $\mathscr{W}$ a set of weak constraints on $\mathscr{D}$, and D an instance of $\mathscr{D}$. The following hold:*

- *given an integer k, deciding whether there is a preferred repair ρ for D w.r.t. $\mathscr{AC}$ and $\mathscr{W}$ such that $\gamma(\rho, \mathscr{W}, D) \geq k$ is in NP, and is NP-hard even in the case that $\mathscr{AC}$ and $\mathscr{W}$ consist of steady constraints only;*
- *given a repair ρ for D w.r.t. $\mathscr{D}$ and $\mathscr{AC}$, deciding whether ρ is a preferred repair for D w.r.t. $\mathscr{AC}$ and $\mathscr{W}$ is in coNP, and is coNP-hard even in the case that $\mathscr{AC}$ and $\mathscr{W}$ consist of steady constraints only.*

Although steady aggregate constraints are less expressive than (general) aggregate constraints, Theorem 5.1 states that both the preferred-repair existence problem and the preferred-repair checking problem are hard also in the presence of steady constraints only.

In this section, we extend the technique presented in Section 4.3 in order to compute preferred repairs for a database w.r.t a set of *steady aggregate constraints* and a set of *steady weak constraints*. This technique is based on a translation of the preferred-repair evaluation problem into an instance of MILP problem [33]. In particular, we refine the transformation introduced in Sections 4.2 and 4.3 by adding an appropriate set of linear inequalities and defining a new objective function, so that the solutions of the resulting optimization problem one-to-one correspond to preferred repairs.

In the following we will exploit the notations defined in Sections 4.2 and 4.3.

Given the system of linear inequality $MILP(\mathscr{D}, \mathscr{AC}, D)$ (see Definition 4.4), we define a new system of linear inequality which takes into account the semantics of the set $\mathscr{W}$ of weak aggregate constraints. Specifically, given a repair $\rho(s)$ corresponding to solution s of $MILP(\mathscr{D}, \mathscr{AC}, D)$ (see Theorem 4.1), we define a mechanism for counting the number of ground weak constraints which are not satisfied by $\rho(s)$. This is achieved as follows. For each (steady) weak constraint $\omega \in \mathscr{W}$ having the following form (see Definition 2.1):

$$\forall \mathbf{x} \left(\phi(\mathbf{x}) \implies \sum_{i=1}^{n} c_i \cdot \chi_i(\mathbf{y}_i) \leq K \right)$$

and for each ground substitution $\theta \in \Theta(\omega)$, we define the variable

$$\sigma_{\omega,\theta} = K - \sum_{i=1}^{n} c_i \cdot \mathscr{P}(\chi_i, \theta)$$

where the summation on the right-hand side derives from the translation of ω w.r.t. θ, as defined in the third step of Section 4.2. Variables $\sigma_{\omega,\theta}$ will be exploited for detecting whether for the substitution $\theta \in \Theta(\omega)$, the weak constraint ω is not satisfied: if in a solution s of $MILP(\mathscr{D}, \mathscr{AC}, D)$, it is the case that $\sigma_{\omega,\theta} < 0$ then the ground weak constraint $\theta(\omega)$ is not satisfied by repair $\rho(s)$. The equations introduced above will be exploited for defining the system of linear (in)equalities $MILP(\mathscr{D}, \mathscr{AC}, \mathscr{W}, D)$ below.

Definition 4.4 *(MILP($\mathscr{D}, \mathscr{AC}, \mathscr{W}, D$))*. Let $\mathscr{D}$ be a database scheme, D be an instance of $\mathscr{D}$, $\mathscr{AC}$ be a set of steady aggregate constraints on $\mathscr{D}$, and $\mathscr{W}$ be a set of steady weak constraints on $\mathscr{D}$. $MILP(\mathscr{D}, \mathscr{AC}, \mathscr{W}, D)$ is a MILP obtained by assembling the inequality in $MILP(\mathscr{D}, \mathscr{AC}, D)$ (Definition 4.4) with the of inequalities

$$\begin{cases} \sigma_{\omega,\theta} = K - \sum_{i=1}^{n} c_i \cdot \mathscr{P}(\chi_i, \theta) & \forall \omega \in \mathscr{W} \text{ and } \theta \in \Theta(\omega) \\ -M \cdot \mu_{\omega,\theta} \leq \sigma_{\omega,\theta} & \forall \omega \in \mathscr{W} \text{ and } \theta \in \Theta(\omega) \\ \mu_{\omega,\theta} \in \{0,1\} & \forall \omega \in \mathscr{W} \text{ and } \theta \in \Theta(\omega) \end{cases}$$

where the constant M introduced in Definition 4.4 is recalculated by choosing $m = |\mathscr{I}| + |gr(\mathscr{W}, D)| + r$ and $n = 2 \cdot |\mathscr{I}| + |var_{\mathscr{W}}| + r$, where r is the number of rows of the coefficient matrix $\mathbf{A}$ and $var_{\mathscr{W}}$ is the union of the sets of new variables appearing in the equations above where $\sigma_{\omega,\theta}$ is defined.

In the above definition, in order to detect if for a substitution θ the ground weak constraint $\theta(\omega)$ is not satisfied (that is, if $\sigma_{\omega,\theta} < 0$), a new binary variable $\mu_{\omega,\theta}$ is defined. The inequality $-M \cdot \mu_{\omega,\theta} \leq \sigma_{\omega,\theta}$ entails that in a solution of $MILP(\mathscr{D}, \mathscr{AC}, \mathscr{W}, D)$, it is the case that $\mu_{\omega,\theta}$ will have value 1 if $\theta(\omega)$ is not satisfied, otherwise $\mu_{\omega,\theta}$ is assigned either 0 or 1.

In order to consider only the solutions of $MILP(\mathscr{D}, \mathscr{AC}, \mathscr{W}, D)$ where each δ_i is 0 if $y_i = 0$ and where each $\mu_{\omega,\theta}$ is 0 if $\sigma_{\omega,\theta} \geq 0$, we consider the following optimization problem $OPT(\mathscr{D}, \mathscr{AC}, \mathscr{W}, D)$, whose goal is minimizing the weighted sum of the values assigned to variables δ_i and $\mu_{\omega,\theta}$.

Definition 4.5. Let $\mathscr{D}$ be a database scheme, D be an instance of $\mathscr{D}$, $\mathscr{AC}$ be a set of steady aggregate constraints on $\mathscr{D}$, and $\mathscr{W}$ be a set of steady weak constraints on $\mathscr{D}$.

$$OPT(\mathscr{D}, \mathscr{AC}, \mathscr{W}, D) := \text{ minimize } (\textstyle\sum_{i \in \mathscr{I}} W \cdot \delta_i + \sum_{\omega \in \mathscr{W} \wedge \theta \in \Theta(\omega)} \mu_{\omega,\theta})$$
$$\text{subject to } MILP(\mathscr{D}, \mathscr{AC}, \mathscr{W}, D)$$

where $W = |\{\mu_{\omega,\theta} \mid \omega \in \mathscr{W} \wedge \theta \in \Theta(\omega)\}| + 1$ is the number of variables $\mu_{\omega,\theta}$ incremented by one.

Basically, the objective function of $OPT(\mathscr{D}, \mathscr{AC}, \mathscr{W}, D)$ entails that it is preferable that some δ_i is assigned 0 (i.e., a database value is not updated) with respect to assign 0 to all $\mu_{\omega,\theta}$ (i.e., all weak constraints are satisfied).

Preferred repairs can be computed by exploiting the following corollary, which extends Corollary 4.1.

Corollary 4.2. *Let $\mathscr{D}$ be a database scheme $\mathscr{D}$, $\mathscr{AC}$ be a set of steady aggregate constraints on $\mathscr{D}$, $\mathscr{W}$ be a set of steady weak constraints on $\mathscr{D}$ and D be an instance of $\mathscr{D}$. Every (optimal) solution s of $OPT(\mathscr{D}, \mathscr{AC}, \mathscr{W}, D)$ corresponds to a preferred repair $\rho(s)$ for D w.r.t. $\mathscr{AC}$ and $\mathscr{W}$.*

It is easy to see that, given an (optimal) solution s of $OPT(\mathscr{D}, \mathscr{AC}, \mathscr{W}, D)$, the value $\sum_{i \in \mathscr{I}} s[\delta_i)]/W$ represents the number of atomic updates performed by any *card*-minimal repair for D w.r.t. $\mathscr{AC}$, whereas the value $\sum_{\omega \in \mathscr{W} \wedge \theta \in \Theta(\omega)} s[\mu_{\omega,\theta}]$ represents minimum number of the ground weak constraints which are not satisfied by any preferred repair.

Example 4.6. The optimization problem $OPT(\mathscr{D}, \mathscr{AC}, \mathscr{W}, D)$ obtained for "Balance Sheet" example, where $\mathscr{AC} = \{\kappa_1, \kappa_2, \kappa_3\}$ and $\mathscr{W} = \{\omega_1, \omega_2\}$ is shown in Fig. 4.2. Herein, the substitutions $\theta_1, \ldots, \theta_4$ are such that:

$$\min(\sum_{i=1}^{20} 5 \cdot \delta_i + \mu_{\omega_1,\theta_1} + \mu_{\omega_1,\theta_2} + \mu_{\omega_2,\theta_3} + \mu_{\omega_2,\theta_4})$$

$$
\begin{cases}
z_2 + z_3 = z_4 & w_{16} = z_{16} - 40 \\
z_5 + z_6 + z_7 = z_8 & w_{17} = z_{17} - 20 \\
z_{12} + z_{13} = z_{14} & w_{18} = z_{18} - 1120 \\
z_{15} + z_{16} + z_{17} = z_{18} & w_{19} = z_{19} - 10 \\
z_4 - z_8 = z_9 & w_{20} = z_{20} - 90 \\
z_{14} - z_{18} = z_{19} & w_i - M\delta_i \leq 0 \quad \forall i \in [1..20] \\
z_1 - z_9 = z_{10} & -w_i - M\delta_i \leq 0 \quad \forall i \in [1..20] \\
z_{11} - z_{19} = z_{20} & z_i - M \leq 0 \quad \forall i \in [1..20] \\
w_1 = z_1 - 50 & -z_i - M \leq 0 \quad \forall i \in [1..20] \\
w_2 = z_2 - 900 & z_i, w_i \in \mathbb{Z} \quad \forall i \in [1..20] \\
w_3 = z_3 - 100 & \delta_i \in \{0,1\} \quad \forall i \in [1..20] \\
w_4 = z_4 - 1250 & \sigma_{\omega_1,\theta_1} = z_2 - 1000 \\
w_5 = z_5 - 1120 & \sigma_{\omega_1,\theta_2} = z_{12} - 1000 \\
w_6 = z_6 - 20 & \sigma_{\omega_2,\theta_3} = 200 - z_3 \\
w_7 = z_7 - 80 & \sigma_{\omega_2,\theta_4} = 200 - z_{13} \\
w_8 = z_8 - 1220 & -M \cdot \mu_{\omega_1,\theta_1} \leq \sigma_{\omega_1,\theta_1} \\
w_9 = z_9 - 30 & -M \cdot \mu_{\omega_1,\theta_2} \leq \sigma_{\omega_1,\theta_2} \\
w_{10} = z_{10} - 80 & -M \cdot \mu_{\omega_2,\theta_3} \leq \sigma_{\omega_2,\theta_3} \\
w_{11} = z_{11} - 80 & -M \cdot \mu_{\omega_2,\theta_4} \leq \sigma_{\omega_2,\theta_4} \\
w_{12} = z_{12} - 1110 & \mu_{\omega_1,\theta_1} \in \{0,1\} \\
w_{13} = z_{13} - 90 & \mu_{\omega_1,\theta_2} \in \{0,1\} \\
w_{14} = z_{14} - 1200 & \mu_{\omega_2,\theta_3} \in \{0,1\} \\
w_{15} = z_{15} - 1130 & \mu_{\omega_2,\theta_4} \in \{0,1\}
\end{cases}
$$

Fig. 4.2 Instance of $OPT(\mathscr{D}, \mathscr{AC}, \mathscr{W}, D)$ obtained for "Balance Sheet" example

$$\theta_1(\omega_1) = BalanceSheets(2008, Receipts, cash\ sales, det, 900) \implies$$
$$\chi_2(2008, \text{'cash sales'}) \geq 1000$$

$$\theta_2(\omega_1) = BalanceSheets(2009, Receipts, cash\ sales, det, 1110) \implies$$
$$\chi_2(2009, \text{'cash sales'}) \geq 1000$$

$$\theta_3(\omega_2) = BalanceSheets(2008, Receipts, receivables, det, 100) \implies$$
$$\chi_2(2008, receivables') \leq 200$$

$$\theta_4(\omega_2) = BalanceSheets(2009, Receipts, receivables, det, 90) \implies$$
$$\chi_2(2009, receivables') \leq 200$$

The optimization problem above admits only one optimum solution where the value of the objective function is 10, as $\delta_i = 0$ for $i \in [1..20]$ except for $\delta_2 = \delta_{18} = 1$, and $\mu_{\omega_1,\theta_1} = \mu_{\omega_1,\theta_2} = \mu_{\omega_2,\theta_3} = \mu_{\omega_2,\theta_4} = 0$. It is easy to see that this solution corresponds to the preferred repair ρ_1 of Example 4.5. $\qquad\square$

Chapter 5
Consistent Answers to Aggregate Queries

Abstract In this chapter, we focus our attention on the evaluation of queries of
a form different from that considered in the previous chapters. Specifically, we address the problem of evaluating *aggregate queries* over data inconsistent w.r.t. aggregate constraints, and introduce a technique for providing *range-consistent* answers
of these queries. The range-consistent answer of an aggregate query is the narrowest
interval containing all the answers of the query evaluated on every possible repaired
database. Three types of aggregate queries are investigated, namely SUM, MIN, and
MAX queries. Similarly to the approach described in the previous chapter for computing *card* minimal repairs, the technique presented here is based on a translation
to the Mixed Integer Linear Programming (MILP) problem, thus enabling well-
established techniques for MILP resolution to be exploited for computing range-
consistent answers.

5.1 Aggregate Queries

In this chapter, we consider a form of queries, called *aggregate queries*, which is a
more expressive than that considered in the previous chapters, where the complexity
of the consistent query answer (CQA) problem is investigated for atomic queries.
Aggregate queries consist in evaluating an aggregate operator (SUM, MIN, MAX) over
the tuples of a relation satisfying the desired condition. In this setting, we consider a
more specific notion of consistency of answers, namely *range-consistent query answer* (range-CQA), which was introduced and shown to be more suitable for queries
evaluating aggregates in [8]. Basically, the range-consistent answer of an aggregate
query is the narrowest interval containing all the answers of the query evaluated on
every possible (minimally) repaired database.

The following example describes a scenario where aggregate queries can be effectively used for retrieving useful information.

Example 5.1. Consider Example 1.3, where balance-sheet data of a company are
automatically acquired from paper documents. The analysis of the financial condi-

S. Flesca et al., *Repairing and Querying Databases under Aggregate Constraints*,   47
SpringerBriefs in Computer Science, DOI 10.1007/978-1-4614-1641-8_5, © The Author(s) 2011

tions of the company can be supported by evaluating aggregate queries on its balance sheets. For instance, in our example, it may be useful to know:

q_1 : the maximum value of *cash sales* over years 2008 and 2009;
q_2 : the minimum value of *cash sales* over years 2008 and 2009;
q_3 : the sum of *cash sales* for both years 2008 and 2009.

Clearly, since the available data are inconsistent, the mere evaluation of these queries on them may yield a wrong picture of the real world. However, the range-consistent answers of these queries can still support several analysis tasks. For instance, knowing that, in every "reasonable" repair of the data, the maximum and the minimum of *cash sales* are in the intervals $[1110, 1150]$ and $[900, 1110]$, respectively, and that the sum of *cash sales* for the considered years is in $[2010, 2260]$, can give a sufficiently accurate picture of the trend of cash sales.   □

In this context, after characterizing the complexity of the CQA problem for *aggregate queries* (such as queries q_1, q_2, q_3 of Example 5.1) in the presence of aggregate constraints, we present a technique for computing range-CQAs of aggregate queries on data which are not consistent w.r.t. steady aggregate constraints. Specifically, as our technique works for *card*-minimal repairs, range-CQAs are the narrowest intervals containing all the answers of the aggregate queries that can be obtained from every possible *card*-minimal repair. We show that range-CQAs of aggregate queries can be evaluated without computing every possible *card*-minimal repair, but only solving three *Mixed Integer Linear Programming* (MILP) problems. Thus, again, our approach enables the computation of range-CQAs by means of well-known techniques for solving MILP.

Throughout this chapter, we assume that the absolute values of measure attributes are bounded by a constant $\overline{M}$. This assumption is acceptable from a practical point of view, as it is often possible to pre-determine a specific range for numerical attributes. For instance, in our running example, it can be reasonably assumed that the items in balance sheets are bounded by $\$10^9$. A discussion on possible extensions beyond this limitation (which could be interesting from a theoretical perspective) is provided in Chapter 6.

5.2 Range-Consistent Answers

We consider aggregate queries involving scalar functions MIN, MAX and SUM returning a single value for each relation.

Definition 5.1 (Aggregate Query). An aggregate query q on a database scheme $\mathscr{D}$ is an expression of the form SELECT f FROM R WHERE α, where:

i) R is a relation scheme in $\mathscr{D}$;
ii) f is one of MIN(A), MAX(A) or SUM(A), where A in an attribute of R; and
iii) α is boolean combination of atomic comparisons of the form $X \diamond Y$, where X and Y are constants or non-measure attributes of R, and $\diamond \in \{=, \neq, \leq, \geq, <, >\}$.

Basically, the restriction that no measure attribute occurs in the WHERE clause of an aggregate query means considering queries which satisfy a "steadiness" condition analogous to that imposed on steady aggregate constraints (see Definition 2.2). Given an instance D of $\mathscr{D}$, the evaluation of an aggregate query q on D will be denoted as $q(D)$.

Example 5.2. Queries q_1, q_2 and q_3 defined in Example 5.1 can be expressed as follows:

$q_1 = $ SELECT MAX$(Value)$ FROM *BalanceSheets* WHERE *Subsection* = 'cash sales'
$q_2 = $ SELECT MIN$(Value)$ FROM *BalanceSheets* WHERE *Subsection* = 'cash sales'
$q_3 = $ SELECT SUM$(Value)$ FROM *BalanceSheets* WHERE *Subsection* = 'cash sales'

$\square$

We now introduce the fundamental notion of range-consistent answer of an aggregate query. Basically, it consists in the narrowest range *[greatest-lower bound (glb), least-upper bound (lub)]* containing all the answers resulting from evaluating the query on every database resulting from the application of a *card*-minimal repair[1].

Definition 5.2 (Range-consistent query answer). Let $\mathscr{D}$ be a database scheme, $\mathscr{AC}$ a set of aggregate constraints on $\mathscr{D}$, q an aggregate query on $\mathscr{D}$, and D an instance of $\mathscr{D}$. The *range-consistent query answer* of q on D, denoted as $CQA^q_{\mathscr{D},\mathscr{AC}}(D)$ is the empty interval $\emptyset$, in the case that D admits no repair w.r.t. $\mathscr{AC}$, or the interval $[glb, lub]$, otherwise, where:

i) for each *card*-minimal repair ρ for D w.r.t. $\mathscr{AC}$, it holds that $glb \leq q(\rho(D)) \leq lub$;
ii) there is a pair ρ', ρ'' of *card*-minimal repairs for D w.r.t. $\mathscr{AC}$ such that $q(\rho'(D)) = glb$ and $q(\rho''(D)) = lub$.

Example 5.3. In our running example, the narrowest range including the evaluations of query q_1 on every database resulting from the application of a *card*-minimal repair is $[1110, 1150]$ (as shown in Example 2.12, the *card*-minimal repairs are ρ_1 and ρ_5; q_1 evaluates to 1150 and 1110 on the databases repaired by ρ_1 and ρ_5, respectively). Hence, the range-CQA of query q_1 is $[1110, 1150]$. Similarly, it is easy to see that the range-CQAs of q_2 and q_3 are $[900, 1110]$ and $[2010, 2260]$, respectively.

$\square$

5.3 Evaluating Range-Consistent Query Answer

In this section, we define a strategy for computing range-consistent answers of aggregate queries in the presence of steady aggregate constraints. Before describing

---

[1] It is worth noting that, as in this chapter we assume that the domain of measure attributes is bounded by $\overline{M}$, *card*-minimal repairs considered here consists of $\overline{M}$-bounded atomic updates.

our approach, we extend some of the complexity results provided in Chapter 3 for atomic queries to aggregate ones. Specifically, the following theorem characterizes the complexity of the problem of computing range-consistent answers of aggregate queries in the presence of general and steady aggregate constraints.

Theorem 5.1. *Let $\mathscr{D}$ be a fixed database scheme, $\mathscr{AC}$ a fixed set of aggregate constraints on $\mathscr{D}$, q a fixed aggregate query on $\mathscr{D}$, D an instance of $\mathscr{D}$, and $[\ell, u]$ an interval. Then:*

i) deciding whether $CQA^q_{\mathscr{D}, \mathscr{AC}}(D) \neq \emptyset$ is NP-complete;
ii) deciding whether $CQA^q_{\mathscr{D}, \mathscr{AC}}(D) \subseteq [\ell, u]$ is $\Delta^p_2[\log n]$-complete;
iii) the above results still hold in the case that $\mathscr{AC}$ is steady.

Hence, the range-CQA problem is hard also when the aggregate constraints are steady. In fact, the loss in expressiveness yielded by the steadiness restriction not only has no dramatic impact on the practical usefulness of aggregate constraints (as explained in the Chapter 2), but also on the computational complexity of the range-CQA problem. We have shown in Chapter 4 how the steadiness restriction can be exploited to devise a technique for computing *card*-minimal repairs. In this section, we show how this restriction can also be exploited to come up with a technique for computing range-CQAs.

In the following we will use the notations introduced in Sections 4.2 and 4.3.

In order to define our technique for computing range-CQAs, we exploit the translation introduced in Section 4.2 which allows us to map a database scheme $\mathscr{D}$, a set of steady aggregate constraints $\mathscr{AC}$ on $\mathscr{D}$, and an instance D of $\mathscr{D}$ into a set of linear inequalities $\mathscr{S}(\mathscr{D}, \mathscr{AC}, D)$ such that every (possibly not-minimal) repair for D w.r.t. $\mathscr{AC}$ corresponds to a solution of $\mathscr{S}(\mathscr{D}, \mathscr{AC}, D)$. Specifically, as in this chapter we assume that measure attributes are bounded by $\overline{M}$, it follows that the one-to-one correspondence between repairs for D w.r.t. $\mathscr{AC}$ and solutions of $\mathscr{S}(\mathscr{D}, \mathscr{AC}, D)$ holds only for those solutions which are $\overline{M}$-bounded.

Corollary 4.1 in Section 4.3 states that the above-cited translation allows us to encode the problem of computing the cardinality of *card*-minimal repairs as an MILP instance. However, as in this chapter we are assuming $\overline{M}$-bounded measure attributes, the value of constant M in Definition 4.1, which bounds both variables z_i and w_i, do not depends on $\mathscr{AC}$ and D. It is easy to see that, assuming $\overline{M}$-bounded measure attributes entails that in Definition 4.1 variables z_i are bounded by $M_1 = \overline{M}$ and variables w_i are bounded by $M_2 = \overline{M} + 1 + \max_{i \in \mathscr{I}} |v_i|$. Thus, in this chapter we consider the MILP problem $MILP(\mathscr{D}, \mathscr{AC}, D)$ where the constant M in the fifth and sixth inequalities of Definition 4.1 is replaced by M_1, and the constant M in the third and fourth inequalities of Definition 4.1 is replaced by M_2. Clearly, these changes need to be propagated also to the optimization problem $OPT(\mathscr{D}, \mathscr{AC}, D)$ of Definition 4.5 which is exploited in Corollary 4.1 to calculate the cardinality of *card*-minimal repairs.

We are now ready show how range-CQAs can be computed by solving MILP instances. The following corollary, which straightforward follows from Theorem 4.1, addresses the the case that the range-CQA is the empty interval (i.e., there is no repair for the given database w.r.t. the given set of aggregate constraints).

Corollary 5.1. *Let $\mathscr{D}$ be a database scheme, $\mathscr{AC}$ a set of steady aggregate constraints on $\mathscr{D}$, q an aggregate query on $\mathscr{D}$, and D an instance of $\mathscr{D}$. Then, $CQA^q_{\mathscr{D},\mathscr{AC}}(D) = \emptyset$ iff $MILP(\mathscr{D},\mathscr{AC},D)$ has no solution.*

Let $q = \text{SELECT } f \text{ FROM } R \text{ WHERE } \alpha$ be an aggregate query over the relation scheme R, where f is one of $\text{MIN}(A_j)$, $\text{MAX}(A_j)$ or $\text{SUM}(A_j)$ and A_j is an attribute of R. Given an instance r of R, we define the translation of q as $\mathscr{T}(q) = \sum_{t:t \in r \wedge t \models \alpha} z_{t,A_j}$.

5.3.1 SUM-*queries*

We now show how to compute range-consistent to aggregate queries involving the SUM function. Consider the following optimization MILP problems:

$$OPT^{SUM}_{glb}(\mathscr{D},\mathscr{AC},q,D) := \begin{cases} minimize \ \mathscr{T}(q) \\ subject \ to \ ILP(\mathscr{D},\mathscr{AC},D) \cup \{\lambda = \sum_{i \in \mathscr{I}} \delta_i\} \end{cases}$$

$$OPT^{SUM}_{lub}(\mathscr{D},\mathscr{AC},q,D) := \begin{cases} maximize \ \mathscr{T}(q) \\ subject \ to \ ILP(\mathscr{D},\mathscr{AC},D) \cup \{\lambda = \sum_{i \in \mathscr{I}} \delta_i\} \end{cases}$$

where λ is the cardinality of any card-minimal repair for D w.r.t. $\mathscr{AC}$, that is, the value returned by the optimization problem $OPT(\mathscr{D},\mathscr{AC},D)$. Intuitively enough, since the solutions of $MILP(\mathscr{D},\mathscr{AC},D)$ correspond to the repairs for D w.r.t. $\mathscr{AC}$, the solutions of $MILP(\mathscr{D},\mathscr{AC},D) \cup \{\lambda = \sum_{i \in \mathscr{I}} \delta_i\}$ correspond to the repairs whose cardinality is equal to λ, that is, *card*-minimal repairs. Hence, the above-introduced OPT^{SUM}_{glb} and OPT^{SUM}_{lub} return the minimum and the maximum value of the query q on all the consistent databases resulting from applying *card*-minimal repairs. These values are the boundaries of the range-CQA of q, as stated in the following theorem.

Theorem 5.2. *Let $\mathscr{D}$ be a database scheme, $\mathscr{AC}$ a set of steady aggregate constraints on $\mathscr{D}$, q a SUM-query on $\mathscr{D}$, and D an instance of $\mathscr{D}$. Then, either*

i) $CQA^q_{\mathscr{D},\mathscr{AC}}(D) = \emptyset$, or

ii) $CQA^q_{\mathscr{D},\mathscr{AC}}(D) = [\ell,u]$, where ℓ is the value returned by $OPT^{SUM}_{glb}(\mathscr{D},\mathscr{AC},q,D)$ and u the value returned by $OPT^{SUM}_{lub}(\mathscr{D},\mathscr{AC},q,D)$.

Example 5.4. Given the set of steady aggregate constraints $\mathscr{AC} = \{\kappa_1, \kappa_2, \kappa_3\}$ and the query q_3 of our running example, $OPT^{SUM}_{glb}(\mathscr{D},\mathscr{AC},q_3,D)$ for "Balance Sheet" is shown in Fig. 5.1. Herein,

- the cardinality of card-minimal repairs λ is equal to 2 (as shown in Example 2.12)
- the objective function encoding q_3 is $\mathscr{T}(q_3) = z_2 + z_{12}$
- M_1 is equal to the given bound on measure attributes $\overline{M}$
- $M_2 = \overline{M} + 1 + \max_{i \in \mathscr{I}} |v_i| = \overline{M} + 1 + 1250$.

$\square$

$$\min z_2 + z_{12}$$

$$
\begin{cases}
2 = \sum_{i \in \mathscr{I}} \delta_i & w_{11} = z_{11} - 80 \\
z_2 + z_3 = z_4 & w_{12} = z_{12} - 1110 \\
z_5 + z_6 + z_7 = z_8 & w_{13} = z_{13} - 90 \\
z_{12} + z_{13} = z_{14} & w_{14} = z_{14} - 1200 \\
z_{15} + z_{16} + z_{17} = z_{18} & w_{15} = z_{15} - 1130 \\
z_4 - z_8 = z_9 & w_{16} = z_{16} - 40 \\
z_{14} - z_{18} = z_{19} & w_{17} = z_{17} - 20 \\
z_1 - z_9 = z_{10} & w_{18} = z_{18} - 1120 \\
z_{11} - z_{19} = z_{20} & w_{19} = z_{19} - 10 \\
w_1 = z_1 - 50 & w_{20} = z_{20} - 90 \\
w_2 = z_2 - 900 & w_i - M_2 \delta_i \leq 0 \quad \forall i \in [1..20] \\
w_3 = z_3 - 100 & -w_i - M_2 \delta_i \leq 0 \quad \forall i \in [1..20] \\
w_4 = z_4 - 1250 & z_i - M_1 \leq 0 \quad \forall i \in [1..20] \\
w_5 = z_5 - 1120 & -z_i - M_1 \leq 0 \quad \forall i \in [1..20] \\
w_6 = z_6 - 20 & z_i, w_i \in \mathbb{Z} \quad \forall i \in [1..20] \\
w_7 = z_7 - 80 & \delta_i \in \{0,1\} \quad \forall i \in [1..20] \\
w_8 = z_8 - 1220 & \\
w_9 = z_9 - 30 & \\
w_{10} = z_{10} - 80 &
\end{cases}
$$

Fig. 5.1 Instance of $OPT_{glb}^{SUM}(\mathscr{D}, \mathscr{AC}, q_3, D)$ obtained for "Balance Sheet" example

5.3.2 MAX- *and* MIN-*queries*

We now show how range-consistent answer to MAX-queries can be computed. MIN-queries can be handled symmetrically.

Given a MAX-query q, we denote the set of indices in $\mathscr{I}$ of the variables z_i occurring in $\mathscr{T}(q)$ as $\mathscr{I}(q)$. Let $In(q)$ be the following set of inequalities:

$$
In(q) :=
\begin{cases}
z_j - z_i - 2\overline{M} \cdot \mu_i \leq 0 & \forall j, i \in \mathscr{I}(q), j \neq i \\
\sum_{i \in \mathscr{I}(q)} \mu_i = |\mathscr{I}(q)| - 1 & \\
x_i - \overline{M} \cdot \mu_i \leq 0 & \forall i \in \mathscr{I}(q) \\
-x_i - \overline{M} \cdot \mu_i \leq 0 & \forall i \in \mathscr{I}(q) \\
z_i - x_i - 2\overline{M} \cdot (1 - \mu_i) \leq 0 & \forall i \in \mathscr{I}(q); \\
-z_i + x_i - 2\overline{M} \cdot (1 - \mu_i) \leq 0 & \forall i \in \mathscr{I}(q); \\
x_i - \overline{M} \leq 0 & \forall i \in \mathscr{I}(q); \\
-x_i - \overline{M} \leq 0 & \forall i \in \mathscr{I}(q); \\
x_i \in \mathbb{Q} & \forall i \in \mathscr{I}_{\mathbb{Q}}(q) \\
x_i \in \mathbb{Z} & \forall i \in \mathscr{I}_{\mathbb{Z}}(q) \\
\mu_i \in \{0,1\}; & \forall i \in \mathscr{I}(q);
\end{cases}
$$

where $\mathscr{I}_{\mathbb{Q}}(q) \subseteq \mathscr{I}(q)$ (resp., $\mathscr{I}_{\mathbb{Z}}(q) \subseteq \mathscr{I}(q)$) is the the set of the indexes of the variables z_i in $\mathscr{I}(q)$ which are defined on the domain $\mathbb{Q}$ (resp.,$\mathbb{Z}$).

Consider the following optimization problem:

$$MILP^*(\mathscr{D}, \mathscr{AC}, D, q) = MILP(\mathscr{D}, \mathscr{AC}, D) \cup \{\lambda = \sum_{i \in \mathscr{I}} \delta_i\} \cup In(q)$$

where λ is the value returned by $OPT(\mathscr{D},\mathscr{AC},D)$. It is easy to see that, for every solution s of $MILP^*(\mathscr{D},\mathscr{AC},D,q)$:

1) s can be obtained from a solution of $MILP(\mathscr{D},\mathscr{AC},D) \cup \{\lambda = \sum_{i \in \mathscr{I}} \delta_i\}$ by appropriately setting the new variables x_i and μ_i of $In(q)$;
2) for each $i \in \mathscr{I}(q)$, the inequalities $z_j - z_i - 2\overline{M} \cdot \mu_i \leq 0$ occurring in $In(q)$ (where $j \in \mathscr{I}(q) \setminus \{i\}$) imply that μ_i can take the value 0 only if z_i is not less than every other z_j (that is, if z_i has the maximum value among all z_j);
3) the equality $\sum_{i \in \mathscr{I}(q)} \mu_i = |\mathscr{I}(q)| - 1$ occurring in $In(q)$ imposes that there must be exactly one i such that $s[\mu_i] = 0$, while for every $j \neq i$ it must be the case that $s[\mu_j] = 1$;
4) considering both the inequalities discussed in 2) and 3) imposes that, if $s[\mu_i] = 0$, then z_i takes the maximum value among variables z_j;
5) the inequalities $x_i - \overline{M} \cdot \mu_i \leq 0$ and $-x_i - \overline{M} \cdot \mu_i \leq 0$ impose that $s[x_i] = 0$ if $s[\mu_i] = 0$. Hence, there is exactly one i such that x_i is assigned 0 in s, and this i is such that z_i has the maximum value among the variables z_j. Observe that these inequalities do not impose any restriction on a variable x_i if $s[\mu_i] = 1$.
6) the inequalities $z_i - x_i - 2\overline{M} \cdot (1 - \mu_i) \leq 0$ and $-z_i + x_i - 2\overline{M} \cdot (1 - \mu_i) \leq 0$ impose that $s[z_i] - s[x_i] = 0$ if $s[\mu_i] = 1$.

On the whole, for any solution s of $MILP^*(\mathscr{D},\mathscr{AC},D,q)$, there is exactly one x_i which is assigned 0, while every other x_j is assigned the same value as z_j. In particular, the index i such that $s[x_i] = 0$ corresponds to a variable z_i having the maximum value among all the variables z_j. Hence, $\sum_{i \subset \mathscr{I}(q)}(s[z_i] - s[x_i])$ results in the maximum value assigned to variables z_i in s.

Now, consider the following optimization MILP problems:

$$OPT_{glb}^{MAX}(\mathscr{D},\mathscr{AC},q,D) := \begin{cases} minimize \ \sum_{i \in \mathscr{I}(q)}(z_i - x_i) \\ subject \ to \ \mathscr{ILP}^*(\mathscr{D},\mathscr{AC},D,q) \end{cases}$$

$$OPT_{lub}^{MAX}(\mathscr{D},\mathscr{AC},q,D) := \begin{cases} maximize \ \sum_{i \in \mathscr{I}(q)}(z_i - x_i) \\ subject \ to \ \mathscr{ILP}^*(\mathscr{D},\mathscr{AC},D,q) \end{cases}$$

Basically, the problems above return the maximum and the minimum values taken by $\sum_{i \in \mathscr{I}(q)}(z_i - x_i)$ among all the solutions of $MILP^*(\mathscr{D},\mathscr{AC},D,q)$. Since the solutions of $MILP^*(\mathscr{D},\mathscr{AC},D,q)$ correspond to the solutions of $MILP(\mathscr{D},\mathscr{AC},D) \cup \{\lambda = \sum_{i \in \mathscr{I}}\}$, which in turn encode the *card*-minimal repairs for D w.r.t. $\mathscr{AC}$, maximizing (resp., minimizing) $\sum_{i \in \mathscr{I}(q)}(z_i - x_i)$ means evaluating the maximum (resp., minimum) value of the MAX-query q among all the "minimally"-repaired databases. As a matter of fact, the following theorem states that the boundaries of the range-CQA of a MAX-query q are the optimal values returned by the above-introduced optimization problems.

Theorem 5.3. *Let $\mathscr{D}$ be a database scheme, $\mathscr{AC}$ a set of steady aggregate constraints on $\mathscr{D}$, q a MAX-query on $\mathscr{D}$, and D an instance of $\mathscr{D}$. Then, either*

i) $CQA_{\mathscr{D},\mathscr{AC}}^q(D) = \emptyset$, or

ii) $CQA^q_{\mathcal{D},\mathcal{AC}}(D) = [\ell, u]$, *where ℓ is the value returned by $\mathcal{OPT}^{MAX}_{glb}(\mathcal{D}, \mathcal{AC}, q, D)$ and u returned by $\mathcal{OPT}^{MAX}_{lub}(\mathcal{D}, \mathcal{AC}, q, D)$.*

Example 5.5. Consider the aggregate constraints $\mathcal{AC} = \{\kappa_1, \kappa_2, \kappa_3\}$ and the MAX-query q_1 of our running example. The problem $OPT^{MAX}_{glb}(\mathcal{D}, \mathcal{AC}, q_1, D)$ for "Balance Sheet" example is obtained by considering the objective function $(z_2 - x_2) + (z_{12} - x_{12})$ over the inequalities in Fig. 5.1 augmented with the following inequalities:

$$
\begin{cases}
z_{12} - z_2 - 2\overline{M}\mu_2 \leq 0 \\
z_2 - z_{12} - 2\overline{M}\mu_{12} \leq 0 \\
\mu_2 + \mu_{12} = 1 \\
x_2 - \overline{M}\mu_2 \leq 0 \\
-x_2 - \overline{M}\mu_2 \leq 0 \\
x_{12} - \overline{M}\mu_{12} \leq 0 \\
-x_{12} - \overline{M}\mu_{12} \leq 0 \\
z_2 - x_2 - 2\overline{M} \cdot (1 - \mu_2) \leq 0 \\
-z_2 + x_2 - 2\overline{M} \cdot (1 - \mu_2) \leq 0 \\
z_{12} - x_{12} - 2\overline{M} \cdot (1 - \mu_{12}) \leq 0 \\
-z_{12} + x_{12} - 2\overline{M} \cdot (1 - \mu_{12}) \leq 0; \\
x_2 - \overline{M} \leq 0; \\
-x_2 - \overline{M} \leq 0; \\
x_{12} - \overline{M} \leq 0 \\
-x_{12} - \overline{M} \leq 0; \\
x_2, x_{12} \in \mathbb{Z} \\
\mu_2, \mu_{12} \in \{0, 1\}
\end{cases}
$$

□

Chapter 6
Possible Extensions and Open Problems

Abstract We here discuss limits and possible extensions of the framework presented in the previous chapters for extracting reliable information from numerical data which are inconsistent w.r.t. a given set of aggregate constraints. Specifically, we discuss possible refinements of different aspects, involving the form of constraints, the class of queries, and the minimality semantics.

6.1 Dealing with Different Forms of Constraints

The complexity characterization of RE, MRC, CQA provided in Chapter 3, and of their variants dealing with steady aggregate constraints, preferred repairs, and range-consistent answers, is still valid for a form of aggregate constraint more general than that used so far (Definition 2.1). In fact, all the complexity results still hold in the presence of aggregate constraints where the conjuncts in the formula ϕ can be also comparisons between variables and constants, expressed in terms of linear (in)equalities (such as $x_i = x_j + 1$). Observe that, in the case of steady aggregate constraints, the steadiness restriction on this new form of constraint imposes that variables occurring in these comparisons cannot be measure variables. This form enables the definition of constraints such as that imposing, in our Balance Sheet example, that the ending cash balance of a year should be the same as the beginning cash of the next year. It is easy to see that also the MILP-based strategies for computing *card*-minimal repairs, preferred repairs and range-consistent answers are still valid in the presence of this new form of constraint.

The form of aggregate constraint can be also changed by modifying the form of arithmetic expressions specified as attribute expressions. This may result in deeply changing the expressive power of aggregate constraints. On the one hand, the expressive power of aggregate constraints does not vary if attribute expressions where addition and scalar multiplication (but not general multiplication) on numerical attributes are allowed. In fact, this form of constraints can be expressed by means of our form of aggregate constraints, where attribute expressions consisting only of constants or single attributes are used. As an example, the constraint $\forall \mathbf{x}\ (\phi(\mathbf{x}) \implies \chi(\mathbf{y}) \leq K)$ where $\chi(\mathbf{y}) = \langle R, (c_1A_1 + c_2A_2), \alpha(\mathbf{y}) \rangle$ can be expressed as $\forall \mathbf{x}\ (\phi(\mathbf{x}) \implies c_1 \cdot \chi_1(\mathbf{y}) + c_2 \cdot \chi_2(\mathbf{y}) \leq K)$ where $\chi_1(\mathbf{y}) = \langle R, A_1, \alpha(\mathbf{y}) \rangle$ and $\chi_2(\mathbf{y}) = \langle R, A_2, \alpha(\mathbf{y}) \rangle$. On the other hand, when general multiplication on numerical attributes is allowed in attribute expressions, the expressive power of aggregate constraints increases. For instance, the constraint $\forall \mathbf{x}\ (\phi(\mathbf{x}) \implies \chi(\mathbf{y}) \leq K)$, where $\chi(\mathbf{y}) = \langle R, (A_1 \cdot A_2), \alpha(\mathbf{y}) \rangle$, cannot be expressed by our form of aggregate constraints. Interestingly, with respect to this extended form of constraints, if, for each product occurring in the attribute expressions, at most one measure attribute occurs, then it can be shown that all the complexity results presented in Table 3.1 still hold and our strategy for computing repairs can be extended as well (basically, this form of products behaves similarly to what happens when the product between a constant and a single measure attribute is used in our form of constraints). On the contrary, in the more general case where products between any number of measure attributes is allowed in the attribute expressions, the complexity results presented in Table 3.1 are not guaranteed to hold. In particular, the repair existence problem becomes undecidable in this case. This can be proved by reducing to the repair existence problem the problem of deciding the solvability of a system of k quadratic diophantine equations, which was shown to be undecidable in [53], for a fixed $k > 2$. The interested reader can find a hint on how this reduction can be formalized in [12], where the repair-existence problem was shown to be undecidable for a class of aggregate constraints less expressive than ours. Indeed, in [12] this result was proved under combined complexity, but an analogous reasoning can be adapted to work under data complexity in our case, by exploiting the higher expressive power of our constraints (which enable conditions relating aggregates evaluated on different relations to be expressed).

The expressiveness of aggregation functions can be increased also by allowing them to be evaluated on the Cartesian product of multiple relations. However, this preserves the validity of the results reported in Table 3.1 (see [25] for details).

Moreover, aggregation functions can be extended by allowing aggregate operators other than SUM to be used. The COUNT operator can be already expressed exploiting the SUM operator (see Example 2.8). In the presence of general aggregate constraints, it can be proved that if only the COUNT operator is used (while SUM is not allowed), all the results in our framework still hold. However, in the case that the aggregate constraints are steady and the aggregation functions use only the COUNT operator, determining the lower bounds of the problems studied in this book remains an open issue. Another open issue is extending the framework to the case that the use of other aggregation operators, such as AVG, MIN, MAX, is allowed in the constraints. In fact, these operators introduce a form of non-linearity, which makes our strategies for characterizing the complexity of RE, MRC, CQA, and our linear-programming-based approaches for computing repairs and range-consistent answers unsuitable.

Finally, an interesting issue which is not covered by the results summarized in this book is the problem of extracting reliable information when the data are not consistent not only w.r.t. aggregate constraints, but also w.r.t. "classical" constraints,

such as functional dependencies and inclusion dependencies. The results stated here
are not straightforwardly applicable to this case, since they are strongly based on
the assumption that no repair can delete or insert tuples.

6.2 Dealing with Different Forms of Queries

It is easy to see that all the complexity results reported in Table 3.1 for CQA and
STEADY-CQA still hold for quantifier-free conjunctive queries, i.e., queries of the
form $Q(\mathbf{x}) = \bigwedge_{i=1}^{n} R_i(\mathbf{x}_i)$. In this case, CQA becomes the problem of deciding, for a
fixed $\mathbf{a}$, whether $Q(\mathbf{a})$ is true in every repair. This obviously boils down to applying
n CQA instances for atomic queries (one for each R_i). Another straightforward extension is that of allowing multiple relations to be specified in the FROM clause of
aggregate queries: this does not affect the results stated in Chapter 5, and in particular the correctness of our strategy for computing the range-consistent query answer.

However, other extensions deserve deeper investigation. In particular, from a theoretical standpoint, it will be interesting to remove the assumption that measure
attributes are bounded in value which has been exploited in the computation of
range-consistent answers. In fact, this removal implies that the boundaries of the
range-consistent answers can be $\pm\infty$: this makes it necessary to revise the strategy
for computing consistent answers and make it able to detect this case.

6.3 Dealing with Different Minimality Semantics

It is worth noting that the framework presented in this book can be easily refined to
work in those cases where it is more appropriate to decide the reasonableness of a
repair on the basis of the set (resp., the number) of digits changed, instead of the set
(resp., the number) of numerical values changed. In fact, intuitively enough, all the
arguments and strategies used to assess the complexity characterization provided
in this work can be easily adapted in the presence of the new semantics working
at digit-level, when a bound on the number of digits of each measure attribute is
known. Basically, in order to deal with this new semantics starting from the results
stated in this book, it suffices to observe that any numerical value with K digits can
be viewed as the weighted sum of K distinct numerical values. Observe that the assumption that the maximum number of digits is known for the values of measure
attributes is natural in many application contexts (for instance, in our running example, the measure values occurring in the Balance Sheets published by small or
medium enterprises are unlikely to consist of more than 8 digits).

In some application contexts, it may be convenient to decide the reasonableness
of a repair by considering the differences between the values in the original and
the repaired databases. This aspect was considered in [12], where *LS-minimal* repairs were introduced, i.e., repairs having minimum LS-distance from the original

database (the LS-distance is the sum of square differences between new and old
values). For the domains of rationals and integers, it is easy to see that there can be
card-minimal repairs which are not LS-minimal, and vice versa. In the specific case
of attributes defined on the domain $\mathbb{Z}$, it can be shown that, in the presence of our
aggregate constraints:

-   the MRC problem is still coNP-complete. Basically, the membership derives from
    the fact that, in order to disprove the LS-minimality of a given repair whose
    distance from the original database is K, it suffices to guess a repair where the
    difference between any new value and the corresponding old value is not greater
    than $\sqrt{K}$. A hint to prove the hardness can be found in [25].
-   for the CQA problem, the same characterization provided in [12] holds in our
    case. That is, CQA is in Π_2^p (since MRC is in coNP), and is Δ_2^p-hard (to prove this,
    the same reasoning used in [12] for characterizing the consistent query answer
    problem in the presence of denial constraints can be used, by properly translating
    the denial constraints used in their reduction into a set of aggregate constraints
    and new relations). Observe that the adoption of the LS-minimality instead of
    the *card*-minimality makes the complexity of CQA increase from $\Delta_2^p[log\ n]$ to
    (at least) Δ_2^p. Intuitively, this derives from the fact that, while the cardinality of
    repairs is bounded by a value proportional to the number of tuples in the database
    to be repaired, a similar polynomial bound cannot be provided for the distance
    of the LS-minimal repairs.
-   since the LS-distance between a repair and a database is not a linear function,
    our strategy for computing a *card*-minimal repair in terms of a solution of a lin-
    ear system of inequalities cannot be exploited to compute an LS-minimal repair.
    Devising a strategy for computing an LS-minimal repair in the presence of ag-
    gregate constraints remains an open issue.

In the case that measure attributes are defined on $\mathbb{Q}$, the authors of [12] them-
selves observed that LS-minimality seems to be unsuitable in this setting. In fact,
this semantics would prefer repairs consisting of many infinitesimal changes of nu-
meric values, instead of repairs changing a much smaller number of values to appropriate (still small) quantities – which is likely to be more reasonable in many cases.
Hence, in this case, when taking into account the differences between the values in
the original and the repaired database is a requirement, a different semantics, which
combines the *card*- and the LS- minimal semantics, is likely to be more suitable.
Extending the framework presented in this book to this case is another open issue.

Finally, the strategies for computing minimal repairs and consistent answers presented in this book work under the *card*-minimal semantics only. It would be interesting to devise techniques enabling these computations also under the *set*-minimal
semantics.

References

1. Abiteboul, S., Hull, R., Vianu, V.: Foundations of Databases. Addison-Wesley (1995)
2. Afrati, F.N., Kolaitis, P.G.: Repair checking in inconsistent databases: algorithms and complexity. In: Proc. 12th Int. Conf. on Database Theory (ICDT), pp. 31–41 (2009)
3. Agarwal, S., Keller, A.M., Wiederhold, G., Saraswat, K.: Flexible relation: An approach for integrating data from multiple, possibly inconsistent databases. In: Proc. 11th Int. Conf. on Data Engineering (ICDE), pp. 495–504 (1995)
4. Arenas, M., Bertossi, L.E., Chomicki, J.: Consistent query answers in inconsistent databases. In: Proc. 18th ACM Symp. on Principles of Database Systems (PODS), pp. 68–79 (1999)
5. Arenas, M., Bertossi, L.E., Chomicki, J.: Specifying and querying database repairs using logic programs with exceptions. In: Proc. 4th Int. Conf. on Flexible Query Answering Systems (FQAS), pp. 27–41 (2000)
6. Arenas, M., Bertossi, L.E., Chomicki, J.: Scalar aggregation in fd-inconsistent databases. In: J.V. den Bussche, V. Vianu (eds.) ICDT, Lecture Notes in Computer Science, vol. 1973, pp. 39–53. Springer (2001)
7. Arenas, M., Bertossi, L.E., Chomicki, J.: Answer sets for consistent query answering in inconsistent databases. Theory and pract. of logic program. (TPLP) Vol. 3((4-5)), 393–424 (2003)
8. Arenas, M., Bertossi, L.E., Chomicki, J., He, X., Raghavan, V., Spinrad, J.: Scalar aggregation in inconsistent databases. Theor. Comput. Sci. (TCS) Vol. 3((296)), 405–434 (2003)
9. Arenas, M., Bertossi, L.E., Kifer, M.: Applications of annotated predicate calculus to querying inconsistent databases. In: Proc. 1st Int. Conf. on Comput. Logic (CL), pp. 926–941 (2000)
10. Barceló, P., Bertossi, L.E.: Repairing databases with annotated predicate logic. In: Proc. 9th Int. Workshop on Non-Monotonic Reasoning (NMR), pp. 160–170 (2002)
11. Barceló, P., Bertossi, L.E.: Logic programs for querying inconsistent databases. In: Proc. 5th Int. Symp. on Practical Aspects of Declarative Languages (PADL), pp. 208–222 (2003)
12. Bertossi, L.E., Bravo, L., Franconi, E., Lopatenko, A.: The complexity and approximation of fixing numerical attributes in databases under integrity constraints. Information Systems 33(4-5), 407–434 (2008)
13. Bohannon, P., Flaster, M., Fan, W., Rastogi, R.: A cost-based model and effective heuristic for repairing constraints by value modification. In: Proc. Int. Conf. on Management of Data (SIGMOD), pp. 143–154 (2005)
14. Bry, F.: Query answering in information systems with integrity constraints. In: Proc. 1st Int. Conf. on Integrity and Internal Control in Information Systems (IICIS), pp. 113–130 (1997)
15. Calì, A., Lembo, D., Rosati, R.: On the decidability and complexity of query answering over inconsistent and incomplete databases. In: Proc. 22nd ACM Symp. on Principles of Database Systems (PODS), pp. 260–271 (2003)
16. Celle, A., Bertossi, L.E.: Querying inconsistent databases: Algorithms and implementation. In: Proc. 1st Int. Conf. on Comput. Logic (CL), pp. 942–956 (2000)

17. Chomicki, J., Marcinkowski, J.: Minimal-change integrity maintenance using tuple deletions. Information and Computation (IC) **Vol. 197**((1-2)), 90–121 (2005)
18. Chomicki, J., Marcinkowski, J., Staworko, S.: Computing consistent query answers using conflict hypergraphs. In: Proc. 13th ACM Conf. on Information and Knowledge Management (CIKM), pp. 417–426 (2004)
19. Dung, P.M.: Integrating data from possibly inconsistent databases. In: CoopIS, pp. 58–65 (1996)
20. Elfeky, M.G., Elmagarmid, A.K., Verykios, V.S.: Tailor: A record linkage tool box. In: ICDE, pp. 17–28. IEEE Computer Society (2002)
21. Fazzinga, B., Flesca, S., Furfaro, F., Parisi, F.: Dart: A data acquisition and repairing tool. In: Proc. Int. Workshop on Incons. and Incompl. in Databases (IIDB), pp. 297–317 (2006)
22. Flesca, S., Furfaro, F., Parisi, F.: Consistent query answers on numerical databases under aggregate constraints. In: Proc. 10th Int. Symp. on Database Programming Languages (DPBL), pp. 279–294 (2005)
23. Flesca, S., Furfaro, F., Parisi, F.: Preferred database repairs under aggregate constraints. In: H. Prade, V.S. Subrahmanian (eds.) SUM, *Lecture Notes in Computer Science*, vol. 4772, pp. 215–229. Springer (2007)
24. Flesca, S., Furfaro, F., Parisi, F.: Consistent answers to boolean aggregate queries under aggregate constraints. In: P.G. Bringas, A. Hameurlain, G. Quirchmayr (eds.) DEXA (2), *Lecture Notes in Computer Science*, vol. 6262, pp. 285–299. Springer (2010)
25. Flesca, S., Furfaro, F., Parisi, F.: Querying and repairing inconsistent numerical databases. ACM Trans. Database Syst. **35**(2) (2010)
26. Flesca, S., Furfaro, F., Parisi, F.: Querying and repairing inconsistent numerical databases. ACM Trans. Database Syst. **35**(2) (2010)
27. Flesca, S., Furfaro, F., Parisi, F.: Range-consistent answers of aggregate queries under aggregate constraints. In: A. Deshpande, A. Hunter (eds.) SUM, *Lecture Notes in Computer Science*, vol. 6379, pp. 163–176. Springer (2010)
28. Franconi, E., Palma, A.L., Leone, N., Perri, S., Scarcello, F.: Census data repair: a challenging application of disjunctive logic programming. In: Proc. 8th Int. Conf. on Logic for Programming, Artificial Intelligence, and Reasoning (LPAR), pp. 561–578 (2001)
29. Fuxman, A., Fazli, E., Miller, R.J.: Conquer: Efficient management of inconsistent databases. In: Proc. ACM SIGMOD Int. Conf. on Management of Data (SIGMOD), pp. 155–166 (2005)
30. Fuxman, A., Miller, R.J.: First-order query rewriting for inconsistent databases. In: Proc. 10th Int. Conf. on Database Theory (ICDT), pp. 337–351 (2005)
31. Fuxman, A., Miller, R.J.: First-order query rewriting for inconsistent databases. J. Comput. Syst. Sci. **73**(4), 610–635 (2007)
32. Gärdenfors, P., Rott, H.: Belief revision. In: D.M. Gabbay, C.J. Hogger, J.A. Robinson (eds.) Handbook of logic in artificial intelligence and logic programming (Vol. 4): epistemic and temporal reasoning, pp. 35–132. Oxford University Press, Oxford, UK (1995)
33. Gass, S.I.: Linear programming: methods and applications (5th ed.). McGraw-Hill, Inc., New York, NY, USA (1985)
34. Gelfond, M., Lifschitz, V.: The stable model semantics for logic programming. In: R. Kowalski, Bowen, Kenneth (eds.) Proceedings of International Logic Programming Conference and Symposium, pp. 1070–1080. MIT Press (1988)
35. Greco, G., Greco, S., Zumpano, E.: A logical framework for querying and repairing inconsistent databases. IEEE Trans. on Knowledge and Data Engineering (TKDE) **Vol. 15**((6)), 1389–1408 (2003)
36. Greco, S., Zumpano, E.: Querying inconsistent databases. In: M. Parigot, A. Voronkov (eds.) LPAR, *Lecture Notes in Computer Science*, vol. 1955, pp. 308–325. Springer (2000)
37. Imielinski, T., Lipski, W.: Incomplete information in relational databases. Journal of the Association for Computing Machinery (JACM) **Vol. 31**((4)), 761–791 (1984)
38. Kifer, M., Lozinskii, E.L.: A logic for reasoning with inconsistency. Journal of Automated Reasoning (JAR) **Vol. 9**((2)), 179–215 (1992)
39. van Leeuwen, J. (ed.): Handbook of Theoretical Computer Science, Volume A: Algorithms and Complexity. Elsevier and MIT Press (1990)

40. Lenzerini, M.: Data integration: A theoretical perspective. In: Proc. 21st ACM Symp. on Principles of Database Systems (PODS), pp. 233–246 (2002)
41. Leone, N., Faber, W.: The dlv project: A tour from theory and research to applications and market. In: M.G. de la Banda, E. Pontelli (eds.) ICLP, *Lecture Notes in Computer Science*, vol. 5366, pp. 53–68. Springer (2008)
42. Lin, J., Mendelzon, A.O.: Merging databases under constraints. Int. J. Cooperative Inf. Syst. **7**(1), 55–76 (1998)
43. Lopatenko, A., Bertossi, L.E.: Complexity of consistent query answering in databases under cardinality-based and incremental repair semantics. In: Proc. 11th Int. Conf. on Database Theory (ICDT), pp. 179–193 (2007)
44. Papadimitriou, C.H.: On the complexity of integer programming. Journal of the Association for Computing Machinery (JACM) **Vol. 28**((4)), 765–768 (1981)
45. Papadimitriou, C.M.: Computational complexity. Addison-Wesley, Reading, Massachusetts (1994)
46. Ross, K.A., Srivastava, D., Stuckey, P.J., Sudarshan, S.: Foundations of aggregation constraints. Theor. Comput. Sci. (TCS) **Vol. 193**((1-2)), 149–179 (1998)
47. Sakama, C., Inoue, K.: Prioritized logic programming and its application to commonsense reasoning. Artif. Intell. **123**(1-2), 185–222 (2000)
48. Wijsen, J.: Condensed representation of database repairs for consistent query answering. In: Proc. 9th Int. Conf. on Database Theory (ICDT), pp. 378–393 (2003)
49. Wijsen, J.: Making more out of an inconsistent database. In: Proc. 8th East European Conference on Advances in Databases and Information Systems (ADBIS), pp. 291–305 (2004)
50. Wijsen, J.: Database repairing using updates. ACM Transactions on Database Systems (TODS) **Vol. 30**((3)), 722–768 (2005)
51. Wijsen, J.: Consistent query answering under primary keys: a characterization of tractable queries. In: Proc. 12th Int. Conf. on Database Theory (ICDT), pp. 42–52 (2009)
52. Wijsen, J.: On the first-order expressibility of computing certain answers to conjunctive queries over uncertain databases. In: J. Paredaens, D.V. Gucht (eds.) PODS, pp. 179–190. ACM (2010)
53. Xie, G., Dang, Z., Ibarra, O.H.: A solvable class of quadratic diophantine equations with applications to verification of infinite-state systems. In: Proc. 30th Int. Coll. on Automata, Languages and Programming (ICALP), pp. 668–680 (2003)
54. Yakout, M., Elmagarmid, A.K., Neville, J., Ouzzani, M., Ilyas, I.F.: Guided data repair. PVLDB **4**(5), 279–289 (2011)